Dublin Gothic

I0141036

Barbara Bergin

methuen | drama

LONDON • NEW YORK • OXFORD • NEW DELHI • SYDNEY

METHUEN DRAMA

Bloomsbury Publishing Plc, 50 Bedford Square, London, WC1B 3DP, UK
Bloomsbury Publishing Inc, 1359 Broadway, New York, NY 10018, USA
Bloomsbury Publishing Ireland, 29 Earlsfort Terrace, Dublin 2, D02 AY28, Ireland

BLOOMSBURY, METHUEN DRAMA and the Methuen
Drama logo are trademarks of Bloomsbury Publishing Plc

First published in Great Britain 2025

Cover design: Jam Art Factory with additional design by AAD

A catalogue record for this book is available from the British Library.

A catalog record for this book is available from the Library of Congress.

ISBN:	PB:	978-1-3506-2085-8
	ePDF:	978-1-3506-2086-5
	eBook:	978-1-3506-2087-2

Series: Modern Plays

Typeset by Westchester Publishing Services

For product safety related questions contact productsafety@bloomsbury.com.

To find out more about our authors and books visit
www.bloomsbury.com and sign up for our newsletters.

World premiere
An Abbey Theatre production

Dublin Gothic

by **Barbara Bergin**

An Abbey Theatre commission

First performed on 21 November 2025
at the Abbey Theatre, Dublin
Directed by Caroline Byrne

Please note that the text of the play which appears
in this volume may be changed during the
rehearsal process and appear in a slightly
altered form in performance.

Ensemble

Karen Ardiff
Jonathan Delaney Tynan
Carolyn Donnelly
Seán Duggan
Emmet Farrell
Clara FitzGerald
Kate Gilmore
Kenneth Hudson
Thommas Kane Byrne
Barry John Kinsella
Denise McCormack
Gus McDonagh
Josuha McEneaney
Dan Monaghan
Penny Morris
Sarah Morris
Áine Ní Laoghaire
Roxanna Nic Liam
Ericka Roe

Creative and Production

Playwright	**Barbara Bergin**
Director	**Caroline Byrne**
Choreographer and Movement Director	**Meadhbh Lyons**
Set Designer	**Jamie Vartan**
Costume Designer	**Madeleine Boyd**
Lighting Designer	**Aedín Cosgrove**
Composer and Sound Designer	**Giles Thomas**
Associate Director	**Éadaoin Fox**
Voice Director	**Andrea Ainsworth**
Producer	**Craig Flaherty**
Hair and Make-Up	**Leonard Daly**

Casting Director	**Barry Coyle**
Fight Director	**Ciaran O'Grady**
Intimacy Coordinator	**Ruth Lehane**

Company

Production Manager	**Michael Lonergan**
Assistant Producer	**Aoife McCollum**
Production Coordinator	**Justin Murphy**
Company Manager	**Danny Erskine**
Company Stage Manager	**Orla Burke**
Deputy Stage Manager	**Barbara Hughes**
Assistant Stage Managers	**Niamh O'Farrell-Tyler**
	Leanne Vaughey
Literary & New Work Dramaturg	**Emily Reilly**
Literary & New Work Projects Coordinator	**Selina O'Reilly**
Head of Costume	**Donna Geraghty**
Costume Supervisor	**Síofra Ní Chiardha**
Costume Assistant	**Eimear Farrell**
Props Master	**Eimer Murphy**
Props Supervisor	**Dylan Farrell**
Head of Lighting & Sound	**Kevin McFadden**
Lighting Operations Manager	**Simon Burke**
Sound Operations Manager	**Morgan Dunne**
Sound Supervisor	**Derek Conaghy**
Marketing	**Muireann Kane**
	John Tierney
Publicity	**Mia O'Reilly**
Digital Engagement	**Eva Louise O'Beirne**
Publicity Image	**Jam Factory**
Literary & New Work Director	**Ruth McGowan**
Artistic Director/Co-Director	**Caitríona McLaughlin**
Executive Director/Co-Director	**Mark O'Brien**

Barbara Bergin

Barbara Bergin is a writer and actor from Dublin, Ireland. Barbara trained as an actor at the Samuel Beckett Centre, Trinity College Dublin. Along with her acting career Barbara has written for screen, audio and theatre. Writing credits include *Love Is the Drug* and *The Clinic* (RTÉ Television), and *On the Couch* (TV3) which she also directed. Plays include *The Bulletin* for The National Archives UK, 14 *Voices from the Bloodied Field* and *Dublin Gothic* for the Abbey Theatre. She is the recipient of an *Irish Times* Irish Theatre Award, an Irish Film and Television Award, a Markievicz Award from The Arts Council of Ireland and a Commemoration Bursary from the Abbey Theatre.

The Abbey Theatre

As Ireland's national theatre, the Abbey Theatre's ambition is to enrich the cultural lives of everyone with a curiosity for and interest in Irish theatre, stories, artists and culture. Courage and imagination are at the heart of our storytelling, while inclusivity, diversity and equality are at the core of our thinking. Led by Co-Directors Caitríona McLaughlin (Artistic Director) and Mark O'Brien (Executive Director), the Abbey Theatre celebrates both the rich canon of Irish dramatic writing and the potential of future generations of Irish theatre artists.

Ireland has a rich history of theatre and playwriting and extraordinary actors, designers and directors. Artists are at the heart of our organisation, with Marina Carr and Conor McPherson as Senior Associate Playwrights and Caroline Byrne as Associate Director.

Our stories teach us what it is to belong, what it is to be excluded and to exclude. Artistically our programme is built on twin impulses, and around two questions: 'who we were, and who are we now?' We interrogate our classical canon with an urgency about what makes it speak to this moment. On our stages we find and champion new voices and new ways of seeing, our purpose – to identify combinations of characters we are yet to meet, having conversations we are yet to hear.

abbeytheatre.ie

A Note from the Playwright

How do you write about Dublin, what can be said that hasn't already been written, sung or sworn? But then again how do you not?

Growing up in a multi-generational family shaped my creative imagination and my fascination with time. Time has been a defining feature of the long road to realisation of *Dublin Gothic*. The story of a myth-busting, loser's history was in my head for years. I tried to peddle it in various forms and formats except the one that it was meant to become. I had TV outlines, a rough radio draft of the first section of Act One, and a half-baked idea of how it might become a piece of theatre. Jesse Weaver, then dramaturg at the Abbey, encouraged me to submit and has been the play's great champion through pandemics and regime changes. Graham McLaren was the first person to say 'I loved it *and*' rather than 'I loved it *but*'. Louise Stephens' graceful and inspiring support allowed me to shape a vast, unwieldy story into the play it would become. Then Covid struck, the world shut down and this epic play about losers seemed destined to get lost in an even weirder iteration of time.

The new Artistic Director of the Abbey Caitríona McLaughlin offered hope, encouragement and delivered the gift of director Caroline Byrne whose contributions, insights and artistic vision have been integral to the play's realisation. Ruth McGowan's energy and focus provided impetus at key moments, driving the play forward. Selina O'Reilly was key to its publication. All the actors involved in workshops and the production took brave leaps to discover and interrogate the stylistic challenges of the text; as always, my tribe. My beloveds, my family and friends have sustained me in all the ways that matter. The loved ones I have lost are in the DNA of the play. My abiding inspiration of course is this city I get to call home, Dublin. Marie and Johnny this is all your doing.

Barbara Bergin

October 2025

Dublin Gothic

A three-act full evening's entertainment

Barbara Bergin

'for my sisters'

Characters

Narrator   *sometimes a single voice, sometimes collective*

Florrie Gately/Ghost Florrie   *30 years old, streetwalker*
* Honor Gately/Ghost Honor   *13–40 years old,*
Florrie's daughter
* Nell Nell Considine   *18–54 years old*
Granny Gately/Ghost Granny   *50, streetwalker*
* Arthur Gately/Ghost Arthur   *14–16, Honor's son*
* Ferdia Meehan   *18–23, Nell Nell's son*
George Doyle/Ghost George   *34–48 years old, Arthur's father,*
writer, lower-middle-class scrounger
Ghost Hibernia Gately   *1916–?, Arthur's daughter,*
Nell Nell's mother

Ned Cummins/Ghost Ned   *30–46, communist, shit-shoveller*
Ghost Sal Cummins   *Ned's mother*
Lil Cummins/Ghost Lil   *26–40, Ned's loyal, depressed, wife*
Josie Cummins   *4–62, Ned and Lil's oldest daughter*
* Frankie Cummins   *14–33, Ned's only son*
* Tiernan Meehan   *18–26, Nell Nell's son*

Bridie Meehan/Ghost Bridie   *40s, tenement dweller,*
general menace to harmony
* Sucky Meehan   *Bridie's son*
* Vincent Meehan/Ghost Vincent   *30s, Sucky's son*
Mamie Boyle/Ghost Mamie   *50s, tenement dweller,*
midwife, alcoholic

* Across the acts the same actors play *Honor/Nell Nell;*
Arthur/Ferdia; Frankie/Tiernan; Sucky/Vincent.

Other Characters

Sir Felton Crothers   *65–82, rack-renting landlord of O'Rehilly*
Parade, dilettante
Dorothy Crothers   *20, Sir Felton's circularly insane niece*

Ninian Drakewell   *24–40, a libertine*
Pierce D'Alton   *33, monomaniacal headmaster, revolutionary*
Ma Flemming   *60, back-street abortionist*
Feilim Fogarty   *16, a schoolmate and Arthur's bully*
Cornelius Considine/Ghost Cornelius   *50s, landlord, tightfist, failed fascist*
Fr. Iggy Rigney   *30s, tenement priest, compulsive gambler*
Valentine Mooney   *30s–60s, singer in Empire Theatre*
Irene Mooney   *mid-20s–mid-50s, Val's wife*
Layabouts   *unemployed observers*
Crooked Prison Officer   *a tenant*
Voluntary Celibate   *a tenant*
Tormented Batchelor   *a tenant*
Dilly   *20s, a chorus girl, hopeful*
Dan Dan   *40s, MC at the Empire Theatre*
Marjorie   *20s, a Hi-Kickette chorus girl*
'Cepta   *20s, a Hi-Kickette chorus girl*
Rita   *20s, a Hi-Kickette chorus girl*
Babs   *20s, a Hi-Kickette chorus girl*
Mr Proudfoot   *50s, solicitor*
Th'Archcleric   *60s, head of the Hierocraship*
Fancy Cunningham   *30s, Irish-American protest singer*
Manly   *40s, a banned writer*
Hennessy   *40s, a banned writer*
O'Buachalla   *50s, a banned writer*
Barman   *in the Carter's Arms*
Tenement Wetbrain   *a patron of the Carter's Arms*
Hollow-Legged Communist   *a patron of the Carter's Arms*
Local Soak   *a patron of the Carter's Arms*
Misfortunate/Ghost Misfortunate   *20s, an unmarried pregnant woman*
Spangles Hedigan   *40s, paranoid stoner, British born to Irish mother*
Flix Kelly   *30s, community activist*
Marcus   *20s, middle-class Maoist*
Maeve   *20s, feminist, journalist*
Dinny Flood   *38–46, TD, minister*

Debbie Al Mostafa   *20, a Southriver drug addict*
Drinker One   *a regular in the Carter's Arms*
Drinker Two   *a regular in the Carter's Arms*
Drinker Three   *a regular in the Carter's Arms*
Young One   *16, local girl*
Southriver Heads   × *3*
Mayo Tom   *20s, a builder from County Mayo*

Future Ghosts

Future Ghost on Segway
Future Ghost A&R Man
Future Ghost in Scrubs
Future Ghost Screw
Future Ghost Prisoner

Minor Characters and Non-Speaking Roles

Act One   French Merchant/Punters/Hewermaster/
Newsboy/Brassers/Shit-Shoveller/Mousie Boyle/Two
Heavies/Desperate Woman/Scholars/Drunk/Peelers/Rebels/
Priest/Firing Squad Soldiers/Screw

Act Two   Emigrants/Mabel/Screw/Lags/Emigration
Officer/Young Fellow/Banished/ Bewildered/Sailor Boy/
American Scholars

Act Three   Sham/Jamesy Lawless/Band Guy/
Angelus Fan/Families Against Patrol/Young Guy/Chef/
Leather Feather Customers/Meterman/Mayo Builders/
Speculator/Screw/Pub Landlord /Prisoners/Addict/
Cameraman/Reporter/Doylesevers/American Tourists/
Doc Slavin Jr/Partiers/Passerby/Bong

Locations

O'Rehilly Parade is a row of tenement houses Northriver. The play takes place at the house, No. 1 O'Rehilly Parade (the home to generations of Gatelys), and various areas within: Honor's chambers, the stairwell, the basement, the privy. The rest of the stage, referred to as the playing area, is where all other locations are conjured.

About the Text

Narrator is the teller of the Gately family history. The characters are unreliable narrators of their own stories, so the Narrator aims to make objective sense of it all. The Narrator is in a dynamic struggle to control the characters, who seek to dignify their actions and take charge of their own stories. The Narrator can be a single or choral voice, depending on the scene. The Narrator is the creation of the author of the story who is not revealed until the very end of the play.

Italicised script is the character's inner voice. The inner voice reveals things the characters won't or can't say aloud. It is how they dignify, justify or repent for their actions. It is also how they get to stay in their own story. Only the narrator hears a character's inner voice, none of the other characters do.

A / denotes the beat where another character continues the line without breaking rhythm.

A // denotes a transition from a character's inner voice to regular speech.

Ghost lines are bolded for clarity.

Ghosts return to fulfil a wish, some wishes are one-time events, others are longer term. Ghosts cannot be seen or heard by other characters, except certain family members. However, ghosts' actions have material effects. The future ghosts who appear in the third act are a new phenomenon to the regular ghosts, making even the dead-world unpredictable and chaotic. There are embodied ghosts, voice ghosts, sound ghosts and trapped ghosts; Arthur and Frankie are trapped ghosts, they can only become free when the truth releases them. Because the ghosts can hear the characters' internal voices, they have more objectivity than when they were alive.

Glossary

Brasser   *Street prostitute, pronounced 'brazzer'*
Churchstate   *The country, post-independence*
Coddle box   *Mouth*
Diddy Parlour   *A snug, a small private area in a pub, reserved for women or those who want a drink in private*
Excape   *Escape*
Galloping Lurgy   *Tuberculosis*
Gunlickers   *Paramilitaries*
Greyshirts   *A failed fascist movement of the thirties*
Hairbaiter   *Troublemaker*
Hewer   *Prostitute*
Hierocraship   *This is the name for the dictatorship of the church; pronounced 'Higher-ocra-ship'*
Kip house   *Brothel*
Opiumistan   *An opiate-producing Asian country; pronounced Opi-um-istan*
Painmelter   *A powerful, addictive opiate*
Rapid-firer   *A premature ejaculator*
Scutterbucket   *Portable toilet bucket*
The Sickness   *Aids*

Act One

Scene One: 'Honor the Virgin'

(*Poke's Alley. We hear the sound of carthorses, barking, whistling.* **Florrie***, 30, wretched, lurks in the shadows. A* **French Merchant** *enters.* **Florrie** *follows behind him.*)

Narrator   'Twas winter 1887 when Florrie Gately took to purse-cutting /

Florrie   *over the pox getting so bad the punters couldn't bear the stench. 'Twas a French merchant in Poke's Alley snared her agin' she reached for his pouch /*

French Merchant   *Arreté, putain*!

Florrie (*grasps her left wrist*)   *He broke her left wrist and gave her two black eyes for herself.*

Narrator   Th'altercation seized up the merchant's palsied heart /

Florrie (*panicking*)   *He dropped dead /*

(*All sounds stop.* **Florrie** *is pulled offstage.*)

Narrator   and the judge sent the six-stone Florrie Gately to the gallows.

(*A noose drops down. We hear* **Florrie***'s muffled scream, then a trapdoor opens, a body swings. Dawn breaks.* **Honor** *(13) and* **Granny Gately** *(50s) by the prison gates. A bell tolls once.*)

Granny   That'll be her. Gone. You're on your own now, Honor, better off for it no doubt.

Narrator   Florrie wasn't much of a mother but she was the only one Honor had and /

Honor   *looking at Granny Gately's sour, wizened oul' mush, she knew she'd never again have anyone take care of her the way Florrie should've.*

Granny   Don't look at me like that, I've done me rearing and can scarce fill me own belly.

Honor   Where'll I go?

Granny   Away down to Tosser's Pot like every wretched Gately afore you and lift your skirts. (*Leaving.*)

Honor   Don't leave me . . . Granny!

Granny (*as she exits*)   Stay away from the hewermasters. And, remember, the pox never lingers on nimble fingers. Advice Florrie should've took, Lord rest her poor ignorant soul.

Narrator   The morning her Ma swung from the gibbet /

Honor   *Honor Gately was 13 year old.*

(*Under the following* **Ghost Florrie**, *noose dangling from her neck, enters, unseen and unheard.*)

Narrator   All Florrie had left her illiterate daughter was the half-baked notion that her father was /

Ghost Florrie   **Highborn.**

Honor   *A gentleman.*

(*A dissonant note sounds.*)

Narrator   Abandoned at the prison gates /

Honor   *full froze and*
half-starved /

Narrator   a life of perpetual poverty and hewering rolling down the hill in front of her /

Honor (*affecting posh*)   *she determined that Honor Gately, sired of greatness, was born for a better life* /

Narrator   than that of a
pox-riddled brasser servicing punters in the coal scut
of a consumptive slum.

(**Honor** *sticks her nose in the air and exits.*)

Scene Two: 'The Hands of Time'

(*Tosser's Pot. Ten years later.* **Punters** *lurk, a* **Hewermaster** *watches, a* **Shit-Shoveller** *shovels,* **Brassers** *loiter.*)

Narrator   Turned out Florrie wasn't yarnspinning about Honor's paternity. Nathaniel Carnell /

Brasser One   Ireland's gentleman patriot /

Brasser Two   had a hankering for back-alley kneetremblers with ha'penny hewers.

Newsboy (*crossing the stage*)   Carnell dead! Read all about it! Carnell Dropsy's Dead!

Brasser One   Dropsy me hole /

Brasser Two   That oul' dirtmerchant gave half of Poke's Alley the pox.

(**Ghost Florrie** *enters.*)

Ghost Florrie   **As Honor's daddy laid in state, his daughter** /

(**Ghost Florrie** *is surprised to see* **Ghost Granny** *enter.*)

Ghost Granny   **marked her tenth year walking the streets by Poke's Alley and Tosser's Pot.**

Narrator   Honor had a reputation among the other brassers as being /

Brassers One/Two   up herself.

Honor   *It troubled her not, she neither sought nor wanted their good opinion* /

Brasser One   just as well.

Narrator   Honor Gately had pleasured fifty men a week for the best part of ten year /

Honor   *and she was still a virgin. If that didn't separate a girl from a hewer, what did?*

Narrator   Her hereditary manual dexterity had allowed Honor to preserve her virginity and her soul.

Honor   *She knew what happened to a body as couldn't dignify itself.*

(*Someone tugs at* **Ghost Florrie**'s *noose; she gags.*)

Honor   *She was fighting for her life* /

(**Honor** *leads a* **Punter** *under th'archway.*)

Ghost Granny   **and it took determination** /

Ghost Florrie   **and more often violence to protect it**.

Punter (*from off*)   Aghhhh, you bit me! You filthy trollop.

Honor (*rubbing her face where he hit her*)   Ya blackguardin' oul' bollix ya!

(*Tattered gentleman* **George Doyle** *enters; he has a strong lisp.*)

George Doyle   Honor! My cursing courtesan. I know not what excites me more, the beauty of your visage or the vileness of your tongue.

Honor   If it isn't George Doyle, come to pay what y'owe me after selling yer novel buke, bechance?

George Doyle   My publisher swears me an advance is imminent. If you could extend me /

Honor   more credit, by way of celebration?

George Doyle   Yes! Soon I'll take my Honor from these squalid streets to the literary salons of Paris

Honor (*relenting*)   Go on with yer velvet verbosities . . .

(**Honor** *leads* **George** *under th'archway.* **Ghost Florrie** *and* **Ghost Granny** *watch them.*)

Ghost Florrie   **Honor had a soft spot for George Doyle** /

Ghost Granny (*cynical*)   **for all his silken words and purple promises** /

Ghost Florrie   he talked to her girl of love /

Ghost Granny (*snarks*)   reared as she was with fanciful notions.

Ghost Florrie (*snarks back*)   A notion gave a body comfort when there was none to be had.

Ghost Granny (*sighs*)   At least George Doyle was a rapid firer /

Ghost Florrie   a one-minute wonder! /

Ghost Granny   and the pox never lingers on nimble fingers /

Ghost Florrie (*ruefully*)   save when the fingers skip a generation.

(**Honor** *emerges,* **George** *follows, insistent.*)

Honor   I'm not that class of girl.

George Doyle   Christ, Honor, you're a hewer!

Honor   And you're a louser, George Doyle, a louser . . . (*She runs off.*)

George Doyle (*outraged*)   You can't leave me like this!

Brasser One   I'll finish you off for tuppence.

George Doyle   Where are you going, Honor? /

Honor (*from off*)   Home.

Scene Three: 'A Slum Called Home'

(*O'Rehilly Parade, stairhead/attic/basement. The* **Tenantry** *are gathered for* **Ned Cummins**' *strike meeting.*)

Narrator   Honor was not long installed in th'attic room of No. 1 O'Rehilly Parade, a four-storey Georgian house situated Northriver. Once the jewel of the Parade, this filthy incubator of deadly diseases was home/

Ned (*speechifying*)   to sixty-seven men, women and childer: all served by a single toilet!

Narrator   The putrid stench from the backyard privy infected the air /

Bridie Meehan   it hung in the hallways /

Mousie Boyle   seeped into the walls /

Mamie Boyle   and crept under the doors.

Ned   A far cry from thc sumptuous grandeur enjoyed by the building's owner, Sir Felton Crothers.

(**Honor** *enters and tries to slink upstairs, unnoticed.*)

Honor   *Since she'd moved in she'd kept to herself. The menfolk leered but the women left her be, except for the trouble-riser from the landing below /*

Bridie Meehan   *who stared her out of it. The vixen.*

Honor   *But 'twas a roof o'er head, so she held her tongue and got on with it.*

(*Attic.* **Honor** *closes her door. Vermin squeak and scratch.*)

Honor   *But alone, behind the door of the freezing, shabby room /*

Narrator   the cost of her living took its toll.

(*Soft discordant violin plays as her 'mist' descends.*)

Honor   *The dreaded mist would descend and she'd lie abed in a swirl of loneliness and ghosts.*

Narrator   A paralysing dread that her life would end as Florrie's did overmastered her.

(*The sound of the trapdoor opening, a swinging body.*)

Honor   *She had no faith to relieve her anguish /*

Narrator   hours melted into days. She shivered in her dark reverie /

Honor   *with only hunger*
and vermin for company.

(*At the stairhead.* **Ned** *is in full flight.*)

Ned   We starve and Crothers dines on our misery! We only have strength if we stand up to the wretch! I say we hold off paying our rent, all of us, together. United.

Bridie Meehan   But he'll pick us off one by one.

Mousie Boyle   Like oul' Jem, thrun out on the streets /

Bridie Meehan   on
account of the hewer Cruthers installed in th'attic.

Ned   Unless we're united that swine Crothers will do as he pleases.

Bridie Meehan   Bouncing up and down them stairs she does be, proudful as you like. The strumpet!

Ned   She brings no punters here, what harm of her?

Bridie Meehan   You'll say differ when Crothers evicts us to turn this place into a giant kip house.

Ned (*losing his cool*)   Over my dead body. You hear me, Bridie Meehan? Over my dead body.

Ghost Sal (*calling from off*)   **Ned?**

(**Ghost Sal** *wanders on, pulling* **Ned** *back in time, to his childhood.*)

Ghost Sal   Nedser?

Narrator   Ned's Ma, Sal, had been a brasser, indentured to a dockside kip house.

(*The grunting sounds of the kip house.*)

Ghost Sal   For the first six years of his life Ned slept under her bed.

Narrator   It gave him a lifelong disgust of hewering, hewermastery and (**Ned** *spits*) the punters.

Ghost Sal   Ned? (*Sadly.*) **He ran away.**

(**Ghost Sal** *drifts off.* **Ned** *leaves the house with his shovel, as if leaving the kip house as a child.*)

Narrator   Ned's working life started at th'age of seven with a manure carter.

Ned (*shovelling*)   *He'd excaped the kip house only to find the same wretchedness prevailed in th'outside world. The rich tret the poor like the shite he shovelled all day long.*

Narrator   By the time young Ned had saved the money to buy his Ma back from the kip house /

Ned   *they told him she'd died of a fever.*

(**Ned** *is bereft. He finds a red book, picks it up and reads as he walks back towards the house.*)

Narrator   By night he taught himself to read /

Ned (*captivated*)   *Marxbuke . . .
the bible writ for the poor.*

Narrator   It gave him reason to hope. Ever vigilant for any opportunity to agitate agin' th'enemy /

Ned (*invigorated*)   *be it the boss, the landlord or any traitor who sought to disunite the overworking class.*

(*Now back at the stairhead,* **Ned** *resumes the tenants' meeting, with even greater conviction.*)

Ned   Hark at me! If we stand united all the tenements in O'Rehilly Parade will join us. The poor will take control of their own destiny /

Bridie Meehan   Ah, there's no need to spit!

Ned   The whole city will join our rent strike and all because of yous. Are we united? /

All   Yes!

Ned   I say keep your rent to feed yisser childer! (*Massive cheer.*)

Bridie Meehan   Get the hewer to hold back her rent first, I'll grant she's Cruthers' spy, Ned Cummins /

(**Bridie** *clocks* **George Doyle** *slinking up the stairs to* **Honor**'s *door.*)

Narrator   Unpopular as the truth generally was, Bridie saw herself as the keeper of it, lending her an unfortunate measure of power in the tenement /

Mousie Boyle   She could hear a flea fart.

Mamie Boyle   Nothing excaped her gawky eye.

Bridie Meehan   *Akin' the johnnie in the velvet topcoat who slunk up to the hewer's lair.*

(**George** *knocks on* **Honor**'s *door.* **Honor** *opens the door, still in her 'mist', she is defenceless.*)

Honor   What are you doing here, George?

George Doyle   I waited these last four days! I'm driven wild without sight or sound of you /

Honor   Quick, get in, afore I'm done for!

Bridie Meehan (*shouting*)   A kip house she's making it into, I tell ya!

(*Door closes. Vermin squeak.*)

George Doyle   *He was taken aback at the poverty of her surrounds.*

Narrator   Yet felt no pang of guilt over always pestering her for credit. Honor /

Honor   *dizzy from days without food* /

Narrator   and a lifetime without love /

George Doyle   *whimpered like a kitten in a drowning sack.*

Honor   Why did you come here George? (*She sobs.*) I'll be thrun out.

George Doyle   *Her mewing was grating on him* // But, Honor, I've come to take you away with me. Tomorrow I shall have the money in my fist. The literary salons of Paris await us, far from this filthy pigsty.

Honor   Oh, George!

George Doyle   There, there, let us lie abed awhile.

Narrator   Believing her nightmare over, Honor leaned into George Doyle and let herself be carried.

(*The basement.* **Ned** *lights a candle to read Marxbuke.* **Lil** *tends to the childer behind a curtain.*)

Narrator   In the dank, mouldering basement, Lil Cummins tended to the fruits of Ned's insatiable appetites, their six tiny daughters.

Lil (*weary*)   *No more than ten months between the childer.*

Bridie Meehan (*shouts from her room*)   You think he'd let her alone, the beast.

Narrator   Lil's body was wracked by constant childbearing, her mind tormented by all they must deny their hungry, mewling brood.

Ned   Once the slums rise up, I'll unionize the Dublin Dung Company! // *The purpose of his life felt so close he could touch it . . . but first, unity.*

Narrator   While th'infant sucked voraciously on her shrunken diddy, Lil mumbled quietly to herself /

Lil   *for Ned wouldn't tolerate religion of any stripe.*

Narrator   As all pleasure slowly haemorrhaged from her life, Lil had turned secretly to prayer.

Scene Four: 'An Uplifting'

(*Split scene: Dublin Bay/O'Rehilly Parade. Sunrise. A steamboat horn, gulls, waves lapping.* **George Doyle** *sails away.*)

Narrator   Despite George Doyle's velvet topcoat and high verbosity, he was no gentleman. The low-grade civilian servant had neither publisher nor anything fit for printing /

George Doyle   *in the eyes of frigid, double-tongued Dublin. Having measured the breadth of his talent against the width of his ambition, he'd found his birthplace wanting. Paris would embrace him, nourish him, liberate him.*

Narrator   He sailed out of Dublin Bay; his mind fixed on his future and all that troubled him of Honor /

George Doyle   *was the stain of her maidenhood still clinging stubbornly to his pizzle.*

(*O'Rehilly Parade, attic. Soft discordant violin plays.* **Honor** *sits bolt upright, knows instantly she's been had.*)

Narrator   In O'Rehilly Parade, Honor awoke to an empty bed and her life's purpose laid waste.

Honor   *He'd took her for th'only thing she had . . .* (*Suddenly fearful.*) *Without it she was nothing.*

(*The violin stops.*)

Narrator   The second split in two, the mist lifted and Honor /

Narrator/Honor   saw herself as others did /

Honor   *The bastard daughter of a murderous hewer.*

Narrator   She was 24, not ready for death yet exhausted by living a life /

Honor   where there was only further to fall.

Narrator   A river of tears, shored up all her livelong days, burst its banks

(**Honor** *describes the scene objectively, seeing herself in context for the first time.*)

Honor   *She cried for Florrie, she cried for her unknown Da, for oul' Granny Gately. She cried for every child hewer this filthy, avaricious city ever spewed forth /*

Narrator   until the river ran dry and exhausted, she fell into a pillow sodden with tears and snot. As day fell into evening, Ned rallied the tenantry.

Ned   From tomorrow no rent is paid to Crothers' lackeys! United we stand! /

All   United!

Bridie Meehan   And what of the hewer?

Ned   Knocked at her door more times to no avail.

Bridie Meehan   She opened her door to her gentleman Johnnie. Seen him skulk out at first light. Happen he's a lackey of Crothers sent to spy on us.

Ned   *Th'oul' vituperator wouldn't cease 'til she had her satisfactions //* I'll call to her now so.

Bridie Meehan   She'll not answer and that'll be your answer Ned Cummins. And mine.

(**Ned***'s footsteps echo loudly as he climbs the stairs.* **Honor** *wakes up.*)

Honor   *She could hear th'oncoming steps, coming to thrun her out. She'd not survive th'icy streets. The kip house would kill her too, only slower. She'd paid up 'til the week's end, she wasn't budging afore then.*

(**Ned** *knocks.* **Honor** *opens her door.* **Ned** *looks up, a light shines down on both of them.*)

Narrator   Nothing prepared Ned Cummins for the sight of Honor /

Ned   *who looked utterly defenceless and completely defiant /*

Narrator   and in that instant he knew /

Ned   *'twas her and only her /*

Narrator   could quench his insatiable appetites.

Ned   *He fixed his eyes to the floor, trying desperately to summon thoughts of his loyal Lil.*

Honor   You've been sent to thrun me out? /

Ned (*looks up at her*)   No, miss! // *As his eyes met hers 'twas all he could do not to grab hold of her, lay her down softly and voyage where the wild seas of their passions would have them roam /*

Honor   What is it you want then, mister?

Ned   I'm Ned Cummins, organiser of the O'Rehilly tenants' strike agin' rack-renting and exploitation /

Honor   The same tenants that'd as soon lynch me as look at me?

Ned   They're afeared you're Crothers' lackey, his spy.

Honor   And what say you?

Ned   I say stand with us agin' him. Prove to them that you're one of us.

Honor   I'll tell you this for yerself, Mr Cummins /

Ned (*passion escapes*)   Ned! /

Honor   Ned. // *He was waiting on her word. For the first time in her life someone was listening to her. It uplifted her.*

Ned   *She still had every one of her teeth.*

Honor (*affecting posh*)   Honor Gately stands alone for she always had to.

Ned   Then I beg Honor Gately to unite with us, with your class.

Honor   I belong nowhere and to no one. Since I was a scrap of a girl I was left to fend for myself and not a body, of any class, threw me a cut of bread nor lifted a hand to help me.

Ned   *Putting words around her sorrow made her defiance all the more noble.* // I was born in a kip house, my own mother a /

Honor   howld yer tongue, mister! // *She would not hear that word on his lips.*

Bridie Meehan (*roaring up*)   Well, what says the hewer?

Honor (*lets rip at* **Bridie**)   Shut yer coddle box, ya oul' hairbater, I'm no hewer!

Ned   *Here she was made human, the satisfaction of his desire.*

Honor   *What was she doing laying herself open afore him? He could only want what they all wanted.*

Ned   *In her panic she went to shut the door on him /*

Honor   *but he jammed his manure carter's boot in the way /*

Ned (*warning*)   look, a gentleman-of-sorts was seen leaving here this morning. Now, I ask you, Miss Gately, if you aim to keep this roof above your head, is that man an agent of Crothers?

Honor   That man is a blackguard who stole th'only thing I ever had to call my own. I curse him and any belonging to him that ever agin' cross the door of this house.

(*The lights flash as the curse is cast.*)

Honor   *She could feel Ned Cummins still standing there /*

Ned   *as if no door had slammed in his face.*

Honor   *A tuft of dried dung from his boot lay inside the threshold.*

Narrator   And as Honor drank in its waft, all thoughts of George Doyle /

Honor   *were swept away like ashes on th'upswell of a winter wind.*

Scene Five: 'Parlour Games'

(Crothers' mansion. St Stephen's Square. **Crothers** *and* **Drakewell***, a libertine, are drinking.)*

Narrator   Sir Felton Crothers' natural impulse was to respond to the O'Rehilly rent strike with a violent mass eviction /

Crothers   *but it annoyingly clashed with his recent conversion //* I have become a humanist.

Drakewell *(laughs)*   Hogwash, Crothers. You are an unrepentant profiteer! I'll wager, you'll crush your wretched tenants' rent strike before the week is spent.

Crothers   I shall make you choke on your words, Drakewell /

Drakewell   better you choke on my cock.

Crothers   *The libertine smiled wickedly and sashayed across the drawing room /*

Drakewell   *inviting a panoramic view of his wildly impertinent buttocks.*

Crothers   *And Sir Felton Crothers vowed to find a humanist solution to the rent strike by any means necessary.*

Scene Six: 'Failure and What to Do with It'

(O'Rehilly Parade, stairhead/attic. The **Tenantry** *wait, fearful.* **Bridie** *prays.* **Honor** *listens in from upstairs.)*

Narrator   Days turned into weeks and Crothers did nothing. The Tenantry's nerve was failing them.

Bridie Meehan   He's torturing us slowly like what th'orientals do. *(Muted murmurs of agreement.)*

Ned   From bottom to top O'Rehilly holds solid!

Bridie Meehan   Just 'cos the hewer didn't pay her rent doesn't mean anything. /

Ned   *It meant everything.*

Honor   *His rent strike had kept the roof over her head. Asides, he'd raised her up, tret her with dignity.*

Bridie Meehan   She's never at the meetings, mind.

Honor   *Since finding out he was a family man she kept a respectable distance.*

Narrator   Noticed his wife didn't look too healthy all the same /

Honor (*ignoring narrator*)   *forced herself to think no more on him* /

Narrator   fixating instead on their common enemy /

Honor   *Bridie Meehan. The menace.*

Ned   Victory can be ours!

Mousie Boyle   Father Feely said if we pay our rent, God will look after us.

Ned (*bitterly*)   Agin' he looks after the childer took out of here in boxes?

Bridie Meehan   God forgive you!

Ned   Can't you see we're winning?

Bridie Meehan   I'll not get thrun out over you trying to get ahead in the communism, Ned Cummins, and I'll hazard I'm not th'only one.

All   Bridie's right / God knows best / C'mon, let's go stand on the street.

(*The* **Tenantry** *disperse.* **Ned**, *crestfallen, makes his way to the basement.*)

Honor   *And in a moment's pass, the wicked shrew ruinated his rent strike.* (*Closes her door.*)

Bridie Meehan (*shouting*)   Don't think I didn't hear you listening, you vixen.

Ned   *Defeat was bred into them that deep, they were afeared to even think on victory.*

Narrator   There would be no uprising of the slums.

Ned   *No Dublin Dung Company strike, nothing in Marxbuke to explain the pitiful life they were damned to now.*

(**Lil**, *a babby on the tit, watches as* **Ned** *hurls Marxbuke into the corner.*)

Lil   *A normal man would've found solace in drink. But Ned swore off porter as child, more's the pity.*

Ned   When my sons are born they'll chase the capitalistic pigs back to England where they belong.

Josie (*from behind the curtain*)   Sorry we're girls, Da.

Ned   *He wished hisself belonging nowhere and to no one, akin her . . . Honor Gately. He felt like choking.*

Lil   Where are you going? /

Ned   The privy . . . is that alright?
(*He leaves.*)

Lil (*blesses herself*)   Our Lord, please let Ned not be at me tonight, that any son might wait. Sweet divine mother, me diddies are all dried up. Hark at how the babby squalls.

Scene Seven: 'Gin Bath'

(*Split scene: O'Rehilly Parade/Ma Flemming's/Crothers'. Privy door creaks.* **Ned** *loiters in stairwell.*)

Narrator   Without class struggle as his lodestar, Ned saw Honor everywhere /

Ned   *most often, when she wasn't there.*

Narrator   Week in, week out he loitered in the stairwell /

Ned   *stewing in the rancid stench of the privy for a glimpse of her, the tread of her foot on the stair or the roars of her at Bridie Meehan /*

Honor (*as she descends*)   I'm no hewer. Never was and never shall be. Amen!

Bridie Meehan (*shouting back*)   Suit yerself but yer not getting fat on food, that's for sure.

Narrator   As ever, Bridie Meehan, trumpeter of the unpalatable truth, was right. Three months after George Doyle vanished, Honor was up Toad Street, seeking out the services of the notorious Ma Flemming.

(*Ma Flemming's rooms. In the playing area* **Ma Flemming** *wheels a screen on.* **Honor** *approaches.*)

Ma Flemming   Now before we start, you'll want to settle the bill. (*She disappears behind screen.*)

Honor   *If Bridie Meehan hadn't put th'idea in her head, she'd never of thought of approaching Crothers /*

Crothers (*enters*)   *who eagerly accepted the whore's offer /*

Honor   *to be his eyes and ears in O'Rehilly Parade.*

Crothers   The rent strike failed but I must root out the perpetrator before trouble rises again.

Honor   There's a ringleader alright, sir . . . one that stirs them all up. (*Whispers to him.*)

(**Crothers** *drops a purse in her hand, exits.* **Honor** *gives the purse to* **Ma Flemming** *and goes behind screen.*)

Ma Flemming   Aren't you an eyeful. Three months gone I'd say. Into the bath and get that bottle of gin down'ya. Then lep up on the table and we'll get rid of your botheration for ya.

(**Ma Flemming** *goes behind the screen, then pushes it off along with* **Honor**. **Two Heavies** *enter the house.*)

Narrator   Sir Felton Crothers wasted no time evicting the ringleader in O'Rehilly Parade.

Bridie   *During the day while the menfolk were out working or drinking.*

(**Bridie** *is shocked when they drag her out.*)

Bridie Meehan   May the divil dance on Crothers' grave . . . leaving a woman and her childer destitute.

(*Interior Crothers' mansion.*)

Crothers   For a pittance the whore's surveillance allowed him to preserve his humanist credentials. Hegarty! Have Mr Drakewell sent for. It's time that scoundrel makes good his wager.

Scene Eight: 'Fever'

(*O'Rehilly Parade.* **Honor** *enters, collapses at stairhead.* **Ned**, *enters, tosses his shovel aside, leaps to her aid.*)

Narrator   'Twas Ned found Honor collapsed by the stairhead /

Ned (*knowingly*)   *reeking of gin, her skirts drenched in blood.//* Can you hear me, Miss Gately? Talk to me! Honor.

Honor (*semi-conscious*)   I'm done for, Mr Cummins.

(**Ned** *carries her up to the attic.*)

Ned   *He'd seen it more times as a boy, young kip house jades bleeding to death or took by the th'afterfever.*

Narrator   As Ned carried her up to the th'icy attic /

Ned   *he could feel the heat of her breath on his neck.*

Narrator   He tried to lay her down on the shabby cot /

Ned   *but she wouldn't let go of him. So he held her close to him as the fever took hold. All through the night he whispered soothing* *incantations . . . willing her not to succumb . . . making promises . . . of a better life to be lived.*

(*Birds chirp, horse hooves sound, lights fade up.*)

Ned   *Afore he knew it, dawn, the hanging hour, came on.*

(**Ned** *slowly lays her down, covers her.*)

Honor (*fevered*)   Don't leave me . . .

Narrator   Already late for his day's work,

Ned   *He had to quit her, tossing and delirious.*

Honor   Don't go . . .

Narrator   Ned descended the stairs /

Ned   *his mind a-swirl on how Lil and the childer would survive without him /*

(*He stops at* **Bridie**'s *open door, looks in the open doorway.*)

Ned   . . . *agin' he noticed Bridie Meehan's empty room.*

(*Puzzled,* **Ned** *takes his shovel and exits. Light floods the attic room as* **Honor** *gets out of bed, wincing in pain.*)

Narrator   Two days later, Honor woke from her delirium with an agonizing fire burning between her legs /

Honor   *and a half-dreamt memory of whispered tendernesses that would not quit her. How she'd got from Ma Flemming's to her bed she hadn't a nun's notion but the roof over her head was safe now. Happen her luck was on th'upswing.*

Narrator   And then she saw it, laid on the floor aside the bed /

Honor   *a tuft of dried dung from a carter's boot.*

Scene Nine: 'Snitchery'

(*Split scene: Crothers' mansion/Tosser's Pot.* **Ned** *stands before* **Crothers**, *who oozes contempt.*)

Narrator   Ned's heart was troubled, his mind confused but his principles led him straight to Crothers' door.

Ned   'Twas me organised the rent strike not Bridie Meehan.

Crothers   I'm afraid your assertion runs contrary to that of my handsomely paid informant.

Ned   Happen your snitch is liar.

(**Drakewell** *sweeps in.* **Crothers** *becomes benevolent towards* **Ned**. **Drakewell** *covers his nose in his hanky.*)

Crothers   Drakewell, this chap came of his own volition to confess he is the instigator of the rent strike.

Ned   'Twas all my doing yet Mrs Meehan and her childer were thrun out on the streets by your brutes.

Drakewell   Hardly a humanist solution, Crothers, you claim victory on false pretences!

Crothers   Merely a tactic to elicit the truth. The Meehan woman shall be reinstated to her room forthwith.

Drakewell   And what humanist punishment for the pungent perpetrator?

Crothers   What would you have me do, Cummins?

Ned   *'Twas surely bait but he was already trapped* // I ask only that my family not suffer for my actions.

Crothers   No more rent strikes, I have your word?

(**Ned** *nods, resigned.*)

Crothers   The humanist, Drakewell, makes a friend of an enemy. I shall reward his honesty with security of tenure for his lifetime. I give you my Englishman's word, Cummins.

Ned   *Lil and the childer'd have a roof o'er their heads . . .*

Narrator   And men disappeared all the time, killed at work, at war, or jumped in the river.

Ned   *The chance of a better life to be lived*

Drakewell   Get gone, you feculent wretch, Sir Felton has a *pressing* matter to attend to.

Ned   But what of the snitch, sir?

Crothers   She is no concern of yours.

(**Honor** *emerges from the archway with a punter.* **Crothers** *and* **Drakewell** *exit.*)

(*Tosser's Pot forms.* **Hewers** *and* **Punters** *surround* **Ned**. **Honor** *stuffs money into her bodice.*)

Narrator   Bound for O'Rehilly Parade Ned found hisself instead at Tosser's Pot /

Honor   *Agin' she saw him, flashes of her fevered dreams o'ertook her . . .*

Ned   *There she was, for all her airs, a tuppeny trick, a back-alley brasser.*

Honor   *Whispered words flooded back. Could it be he'd come for her? If so, she'd a mind to go with him.*

Ned   *His innards heaved as she moved toward him. Crothers' snitch.* (*Spits and walks away.*)

Honor   *Her cheeks burned with a scalding shame* /

Narrator   swift overtook by th'instinct to raise herself above *it* /

Honor   *The shit-shovelling son of a kip house hewer, who was he to scorn her?* /

(**Ghost Granny** *and* **Ghost Florrie** *come from under the archway.*)

Ghost Florrie   **the daughter of a gentleman.**

Honor   *Let Ned Cummins think as he may, what George Doyle done to her didn't make her a hewer.*

Ghost Granny   Hewers never gave it away for free.

Scene Ten: 'Babyangelcakes'

(*Split scene: O'Rehilly Parade/Tosser's Pot. Basement.* **Ned** *paces. Behind the curtain, a babby cries,* **Lil** *retches.*)

Narrator   Every principle Ned Cummins lived his life by demanded he expose Honor Gately's snitchery. Yet, weeks passed, a month /

Ned (*defensive*)   *He was biding his time* /

Narrator   his silence tormented him.

(**Ned** *takes his shovel and makes his way to the privy.* **Lil** *emerges wiping vomit from her mouth.*)

Narrator   'Twas over three months since Ned had troubled Lil, so she was well on her way.

Lil   *This one'll take me with it. Feeding on my flesh, sucking the life blood out of me. And for what? Only to bring forth another face twisted all out of shape from wanting.*

Bridie Meehan   Lil Cummins wasn't th'only tenant in the family way, mind.

Narrator   Ma Flemming's painful procedure had failed to purge Honor of George Doyle's parting gift.
But as Honor's babby grew inside her, the body she'd always had to defend /

Honor   *took charge of itself, it told her what to do. And it was making someone for her.*

Narrator   She started believing, and 'twasn't faith in God, for Honor had none.

Honor   *'Twas faith in herself. She'd been right about everything, even him. He'd proved hisself no differ than all the rest in the finish.*

Narrator   She was twenty-five-year old /

Honor   *still had all her teeth* /

Narrator   and soon /

Honor   *she would be alone no longer.*

(**Honor** *sticks her nose in the air, leaves.* **Lil** *sees* **Honor** *pass and* **Ned** *following behind her at a distance.*)

Narrator   By summer Honor had blossomed like a wild-flower meadow.

Ned   *Her cheeks flushed pink, her lips reddened, her hair fell about her luminous face like a soft satin curtain.*

(*Tosser's Pot forms.* **Punters** *wait in line for* **Honor** *as she eats an angel cake.* **Brassers** *watch.*)

Narrator   Demand for her services multiplied.

Brasser One   She was going through gloves faster than the gallopin' pox in a kip house.

Honor   *And with the money she fed her swelling belly all manner of grub she'd never had. Fish and soft bread. Cuts of meat. And angel cake, so much angel cake that she fixed on calling her babby . . . Angelica.*

Narrator   As her beauty intensified so did Ned's torment.

Ned   *Worse than the snitch, he was the snitch's keeper.*

Narrator   The choice he couldn't make had made itself anyway.

Ned   *He loved her and there was nothing he could do save hate himself for it. He couldn't face going home.*

Narrator   Though he'd neither taste nor inclination for porter, he sought solace in the Carter's Arms.

(**Ned** *holds the drink in front of him, then with a flourish throws his head back as he drinks it all in one go.*)

Lil   *He looks at me now like an unpaid debt, a nagging reminder of what he owes but cannot pay. And she, the one his eye has turned to, ripens and blossoms as her shame grows. Her belly swollen with her hewer's issue.*

Scene Eleven: 'Birthing a Century'

(*O'Rehilly Parade. Fireworks, sounds of people cheering.*)

Narrator   As the century drew to a close Southriver, fireworks lit up the night sky. Northriver, in O'Rehilly Parade a struggle of a more visceral nature was apace. Midwife Mamie Boyle /

Mamie Boyle   *had been dug out of the diddy parlour in the Carter's and, half-shot, was running 'twixt the hewer above on her first and Lil Cummins below on her seventh . . . not that you'd know it.* // Lil, you'll make it harder holding on, the little scrap will get born one ways or th'other.

Narrator   Upstairs, Honor was embracing her labour with relish.

Honor   *For the first time in her sorry life pain had meaning.*

(*Bells ring, cheering, fireworks as the new century begins.* **Ned** *makes his way up from the basement.*)

Narrator   Honor pushed Angelica out as the bells rang in the new century. Mamie handed her the giant babby

Honor   Ohh . . . She's . . . she's /

Mamie Boyle   a boy. God bless her. A huge boy.

Ned (*appears at door*)   Mamie, Lil says she's dying and the child with her.

Mamie Boyle   Sweet suffering saviour . . . I'll go to her, fetch a sup of water for the new mammy there.

Narrator   Honor's heart exploded with love as she cooed at her giant infant made of angel cakes.

Ned   *She never peeled her eyes from the babby to acknowledge him. He felt a badness swell in him.*

Honor (*besotted*)   Come look at him, my beautiful Arthur.

Ned   That sounds like a nob's name.

Honor   As well it may, for my Arthur will be a gentleman like /

Ned   his father? The kind who'd sire his bastard from a tuppeny trick // *The words were hardly out when he wished them in again. Tearing her eyes from the suckling babe she fixed her defiant gaze on him.*

Honor   Get out.

Ned   *And with that, he was demoted to the ranks, someone else to stick her nose up at.*

Narrator   As Ned descended to the basement an unmerciful roar issued forth from Lil.

Lil (*spent*)   *And unto Ned Cummins was delivered his long-awaited son.*

Mamie Boyle   *Born in his caul* // Two babbies brought forth and the century only an hour in. (*Coughs.*) I'm away to the Carter's to sink a gallon of porter.

Ned   Of course, sorry, Mamie, here you go. (*Gives her some coins.*)

Mamie Boyle   *She said nothing about the caul, it'd fetch a guinea from th'Egyptian apothecary in Poke's Alley.*

Lil   He's called Frankie, for me dead brother.

Narrator   Lil handed Ned his son.

Lil   *Searched his eyes for what wasn't there* /

Narrator   afore she turned to the wall and surrendered to her loveless fate.

The babby squalled, Ned looked at little Frankie Cummins /

Ned   *the tiny infant looked like a rat.*

Scene Twelve: 'Rising Sons'

(Split scene: street/O'Rehilly Parade/Carter's Arms. 1914. Marching, horses, a car horn. **Frankie** *hawks his papers.)*

Narrator   1914. War had broke out in Europe.

Frankie   HERALD OR BUGLE! MA FLEMMING ARRESTED!

Narrator   14-year-old Frankie Cummins sold more newspapers than all the capital's newsboys put together.

Lil *(lifeless)   The family crust winner since his father Ned gave hisself over wholly to the porter.*

Josie   *Their mother, Lil, scarce more use than a breathing shroud /*

Frankie   *and his sister, Josie, blacklisted /*

Josie   *for strike weaving /*

Lil   *Ned's neglected family had long looked to /*

Frankie   *the son he tret like shite on a carter's boot to feed them. //* HERALD OR BUGLE!

Narrator   Hawking papers from dawn 'til duskfall, he'd come home /

Frankie   *to the welcome of his Da's drunken maulers*

(Basement. **Frankie** *descends. Sound of* **Ned***'s bootsteps. Shadows move, dull thumps sound as speaks.)*

Frankie   *When the bateing was done, he'd curl up behind the scutterbucket and cry hisself to sleep, while above his very head, that blubberpuss of a sissy, Arthur Gately, lived akin a prince.*

(Ground-floor chambers. **Honor** *dotes on* **Arthur**, *who speaks with a lisp, like his father* **George Doyle***.)*

Narrator   Lavishing her son with all she'd ever lacked, Honor cocooned Arthur from slum life.

Honor   *He spent his days in their chambers eating angel cake /*

Arthur (*precociously*)   *and reading voraciously.*

Honor   *He could use words she'd never heard of!*

Narrator   But born as he was into someone else's story, the greatest work of fiction Arthur Gately swallowed was Honor's creation.

(*A dissonant note sounds. The* **Narrator**, *now focused on* **Arthur** *and* **Frankie** *is more dismissive of* **Honor**.)

Arthur   *The tragedy of his dead father. Lost at sea afore he was born.*

Narrator   Trust being the liar's stock, authenticity was the trade. Honor was not herself to her son.

Honor (*defiant*)   *She was someone better.*

Narrator   Her streetwalking days long behind her, Sir Felton Crothers had installed her /

Honor   *in the front chambers, in exchange for collecting his rent off the tenantry /*

Bridie Meehan   th'avaricious strumpet.

Honor   *In revengeance, Bridie turned her little gouger of a son, Sucky, agin' Arthur.*

Sucky Meehan (*from off, he sings*)   Blubberpuss, he has no Da . . .

Honor   *While she herself took pride in the tenantry's despisement of her, sufferin' their grudgery on an innocent child only further hardened her agin' them. In the finish, she done what she had to /*

(**Honor** *puts a cap on* **Arthur** *and leads him to the front door.*)

Arthur (*shocked*)   *and enrolled him as a boarder in St Eithne's School for Young Gaels.*

Honor   *He ran away more times /*

Arthur   *but she always sent him back /*

Honor   *For she knew you'd forget a lonely childhood in a way you'd never forget a hungry one.*

Arthur   *But what was loneliness if not a hunger of the soul?* (*He exits.*)

Narrator   Honor missed him profoundly but the bettering of Arthur was her rebuke to Ned Cummins /

Honor   *and all who'd thought her nothing better than a tuppeny trick.*

(*The Carter's Arms forms.*)

Narrator   For Ned's part, he waged his war in the Carter's Arms. Sat aside Mamie Boyle in the diddy parlour /

Ned   *he drank to unremember.*

Narrator   Floating in a sea of porter, he could unremember his famished family /

Ned   *unremember every shovel of shite . . . but he could never unremember her /*

Honor   *nor she him. Only once, when the wave of his tenderness washed over her, had she belonged in her own life. But their love had been all out of time and no way of imagining could a body find to see how it'd ever come to pass.*

Narrator   Life had limped on, they'd taken refuge in their difference, shored up their disappointed hearts /

All   and made life a living hell for all who weren't the other.

Scene Thirteen: 'Determination'

(*Split scene: St Eithne's School/O'Reilly Parade. Arthur, bored, as fellow* **Scholars** *listen devotedly to* **Pearse D'Alton**.)

Narrator   Pearse D'Alton, commander-in-chief at St Eithne's School was educating his young Gaels /

D'Alton   to liberate themselves
from the shackles of Empire!

(**Scholars** *cheer while* **Arthur** *yawns loudly.*)

Narrator   Arthur Gately was a highly precocious and
deeply unpopular scholar.

Arthur   *Each day at St Eithne's ushered in fresh torment. He
endured constant ridicule for* /

Scholar One   his lisping slum accent /

Scholar Two   his hatred
of sports /

Feilim Fogarty   his likeness to Nathaniel Carnell! (**Scholars**
laugh.)

Arthur   *The dead patriot who embodied the lofty hopes and plain
looks of his people.*

Narrator   By his fifteenth birthday an angry rash of red
pusthules took possession of his brow.

Arthur (*his voice breaking as he speaks*)   *His voice deepened and
his moods darkened.*

(*O'Rehilly Parade.* **Frankie** *stands between O'Rehilly and
St Eithne's.* **Honor** *and* **Arthur** *look out into the abyss.*)

Frankie   *Agin' Blubberpuss came home on his holliers* /

Honor   *she couldn't
relaxify herself to th'alterations in him.*

Arthur   Really, Mother, must you insist on grinning at me
like an imbecile.

Narrator   And so the gap 'twixt mother and son yawned
ever wider. Once back in the dormitory of St Eithne's /

Arthur   *he'd
chastiste himself for belittling her, for squandering the soothing balm
of her adoration.*

Narrator   While in her empty rooms she wept softly /

Honor   *to think how she shamed him.*

(*A* **Desperate Woman** *enters.* **Bridie Meehan** *and* **Mamie Boyle** *chatter on the stairwell.*)

Narrator   How Honor provided so well for her son was the source of predictable speculation /

Mamie Boyle   Scarce leaving her rooms and only women darkening her door.

Bridie Meehan   Procuring virgins for Crothers and his ilk, the voluptuary.

Narrator   But Honor's wretched callers /

Honor   *had, by force or consequence, already been relieved of their virtue.*

Narrator   Honor's decision to send Arthur to St Eithne's had been made possible /

Honor   *by determination.* (*She pulls across* **Ma Flemming***'s screen.*) *The first one was tricky but she soon learned the knack.*

Narrator   In Honor, desperate women from all over the city found a measure of mercy /

Honor   *and a softer touch than Ma Flemming, at whose hands she herself had near expired.*

Narrator   Honor's purse bulged and the source of her funds remained a mystery.

Honor   *Shame being the best secret keeper of all. Moreover, as Crothers' rent collector /*

(**Honor** *opens her door,* **Bridie** *and* **Mamie** *scatter.*)

Bridie Meehan   the tenantry were that occupied avoiding the turncoat trollop /

Honor   *they hadn't half a notion of her secret occupation.*

(**Honor** *shows the* **Desperate Woman** *out,* **Frankie** *enters hawking his papers.*)

Frankie   BUGLE OR HERALD! MA FLEMMING ON TRIAL!

Honor   *Asides, the ranks of th'unwanted and unloved needed no swelling. She'd only to look at little Frankie Cummins for reminding of that.*

(**Honor** *goes back inside.* **Frankie** *watches* **Desperate Woman** *gingerly walk off, holding the railings for support.*)

Narrator   But 'Little Frankie Cummins' had latterly noticed something about Honor's visitors.

Frankie   *They were all a-jitter. Blubberpuss Gately wasn't th'only kid in O'Rehilly who could read. With the newspapers full of Ma Flemming's trial, he done the mathematicals.* (*Knocks for* **Honor**.)

Honor   Frankie, are you alright, son?

Frankie   I know what you're doing, Ma Gately.

Honor   *If shame swore a secret, hunger sold it for tuppence. But she'd not come this far to be undone by a malignant little scut whose hunger'd never be sated* /

Franike   *She reefed him inside, squared up to him* /

Honor   Squeal on me and the pittance the peelers'll pay ya, your Da'll squander in a night in the Carter's . . . and who'll suffer the sting of that? Who?

Frankie   *She let go of him, walked to the window. Without turning her dial to look at him she laid out the plan.*

(*Streetscape forms as* **Frankie**, *full of purpose, navigates through it.*)

Frankie   *He knew every back alley, long lane and cut-through in the city* // HERALD OR BUGLE!

Desperate Woman   I'll take *The Leader*, son.

Frankie   A penny. Folly behind me, ma'am. // *Changing routes regular, he'd lead them Northriver to O'Rehilly Parade. Agin' Miss Honor was done with them, he'd fetch a carriage to take them away.* //

HERALD OR BUGLE! MA FLEMMING TO HANG!

Narrator   Despite Honor's adept handling of the matter /

Honor   *it discommoded her to bethink how easy a body's world could fall away to nothing . . . for the little clype had her in his grip.*

Frankie   *Nobody'd ever been scarified of him afore. He liked the feel.*

Honor   *There were men a-plenty about the parade found harbour from their hopelessness in the tormenting of a woman defenceless. He wouldn't be short on learning.*

(*The faint sound of the discordant violin begins.*)

Narrator   For the first time since Arthur was born the dreaded mists began to descend on her again.

Scene Fourteen: 'Dorothy'

(*Crothers'.* **Crothers**, **Dorothy**, **Drakewell** *sit in silence.* **Dorothy** *plays with a charm bracelet on her left wrist.*)

Narrator   Dorothy Crothers' greatest wish was to live an independent life.

Crothers   *He'd promised to have his niece married by Michelmas but with the war taking all the men away . . .*

Dorothy   Uncle Felton, I must excuse myself, the journey from London has fatigued me.

Crothers   My dear, Mr Drakewell has made quite the journey of his own to make your acquaintance.

Drakewell   *She put him in mind of a cow looking through a hedge //* It's not too early for cognac is it?

Crothers   *The aging libertine cut a pathetic figure, his painted hair scarcely covering his shining pate.*

Drakewell   Your uncle tells me you are a keen collector of charms for your bracelet, Miss Crothers.

Dorothy (*sighing, then speaking rapidly*)   I am also a social reformer, birth control advocate, a private intellectual, a hunter, theosophist, speaker of Mandarin and a suffragist.

Drakewell   Ah! Then you can settle a matter which has long perplexed me. How is it these champions of women's rights are so often the very women whom nature has wronged?

Dorothy   Really, Uncle, if this is the kind of lame-brained discourse I'm expected to engage in, I insist upon retiring. I am a-blood at present and shall leave you to your cattle trading. (*She leaves.*)

Drakewell   She speaks her mind.

Crothers   Ah, her mind . . . not only is she unlovely. Dorothy suffers from circular insanity.

Drakewell (*fondly*)   My first wife was circularly insane and, in her maniacal moods, gloriously uninhibited

Crothers   And tell me, Drakewell, what of your Egyptian creditor, is he to be reasoned with?

Drakewell   *Thoughts of how Al Mostafa settled unpaid debts brought a hot sweat to his brow* /

Crothers   *and the paint on his scalp ran in black rivulets toward his eyes, like a waterfall of doom*

Drakewell   Michelmas, you said?

Scene Fifteen: 'Gaelscoil'

(*St Eithne's School.* **D'Alton** *paces, thinking.* **Arthur** *sighs loudly, the* **Scholars** *ignore him.*)

Narrator   The terms dragged by at St Eithne's and Arthur Gately's expansive intellect was being laid waste.

D'Alton   *War on foreign fields had turned Empire's eyes away from Ireland* // Drilling will replace history, street fighting in place of Mathematics.

Arthur   Is every lesson to be war games?

Scholar   Shut up, Gately, you fat oaf.

D'Alton   The tyranny of the Enemy Empire is . . . Feilim?

Feilim Fogarty   Drenched in the blood of the Gaels and can only end in revolution!

Arthur   What exactly is revolutionary about the exploitation of half-formed young men too stupid to think for themselves by those in pursuit of power?/

D'Alton   Freedom!
Gately, Freedom

Arthur   But after freedom, who will hold the power then?

D'Alton   The Gaels, of course.

Arthur   But which Gaels?

D'Alton   You may have that out with your fellow scholars, Gately, while I fetch the weaponry.

(**D'Alton** *leaves, smiling at* **Fogarty** *as he does.* **Fogarty** *closes in on* **Arthur**.)

Feilim Fogarty   Did you call us stupid, Gately?

Arthur   No. I called you stupid *and* half-formed.

(*Lightning quick* **Fogarty** *punches* **Arthur** *in the jaw. He reels backwards, then doubles forward.*)

Narrator   Pain seared through Arthur's jaw. The second split in two.

(*The* **Scholars** *and* **Feilim** *encircle* **Arthur**. **Arthur** *walks out of the circle, he watches as they assault him.*)

Arthur   *He migrated from himself, observing himself from afar /*

Narrator/Arthur   He saw himself as others did.

Arthur   *. . . a helpless, human kick-bag. Long ago pains surged through him. How often he'd been wrenched from childhood slumbers by the cries of Frankie Cummins below or the shrieks of Bridie Meehan above.*

(*We hear* **Frankie** *and* **Bridie** *cry out.*)

Arthur   *And how, in the dull silences that followed, he could not sleep for knowing that when their bitter tears had dried, before their bruises had yellowed, it would be an over-sized, fatherless child on whom they'd vent their vagrant spleen. No more for Arthur Gately the wearing of some brute's second-hand shame.*

Narrator   He stood up, fists pulsing, demanding vengeance.

Arthur   *Any imbecile could see that he was physically capable of flattening the snarling Feilim Fogarty.*

Scholars   Fight! Fight! Fight!

Narrator   One decent uppercut could change everything for Arthur.

Arthur   *But he abhorred physical violence, it was the province of cowards. Besides, he neither sought nor wanted their good opinion.*

(**Arthur** *lets his fists go limp, retreats. The* **Scholars** *make chicken sounds.* **D'Alton** *returns.*)

D'Alton   This, my young Gaels, is the C96 semi-automatic. Wipe your face, Gately, you're bleeding.

Arthur   Feilim Fogarty punched me in the jaw.

D'Alton   The proud young Gael savours the taste of his own blood.

(**D'Alton**, *delighted with his protégé, hands* **Fogarty** *the gun; his bootlickers gather round enviously.*)

Narrator   The pus in Arthur's pimples boiled with injustice. Because D'Alton knew /

Arthur   *he had no angry father to account to, he would let the brute Fogarty do as he liked.*

Narrator   The belief that he was arbitrarily cursed took up residence in Arthur Gately's enormous soul.

Scene Sixteen: 'Bad Penny'

(*O'Rehilly Parade.* **Honor***'s ground-floor chambers.* **George Doyle***, ravaged by pox and poverty, faces* **Honor**.)

Narrator   Sixteen year after he'd swindled Honor of her maidenhead, George Doyle stood afore her /

Honor   *Ragged, stinking and hollow-eyed, akin something dug up from a charnel ground.*

George Doyle   I never stopped thinking of you, Honor.

Honor   *Crothers' rent money lay scarce hid, in arm's reach of the dirty article.* (*She slips it into her bodice.*) *There was nothing of him in Arthur, save the lisp.*

George Doyle   This is for you. My *Novelbuke*. (*Offering her a tattered book.*)

Honor   *And her unable to read.* // What do you want, George Doyle?

George Doyle   Relief. The sweet relief only you can deliver, Honor.

Honor   *He was riddled to high hell with the pox!* // You have to leave.

George Doyle (*incredulous*)   You deny me? After I dedicated my life's work to you? (*Waving book.*) For this, I exiled myself, lived as a troglodyte, sought refuge in absinthe and the cursed fireships of Le Quartier Rouge. Until, at last, Paris repulsed me even more than my own city, for only then could I write. And, in writing, come to love what I hated most, Dublin.

Honor   *The syph was gone to his brain.*

George Doyle   Once Dublin solicited me, I yearned only for the greatest of my life's pleasures, your dextrous digits about my pizzle. My Soliticitus Honoré. My final chapter.

Kids (*off, singing*)

  Blupperpuss, he has no Da

Honor (*panics*) *Why were the childer singing and Arthur off at school? He hadn't run away again?*

(**Bridie Meehan** *and* **Mamie Boyle** *enter from the privy with their chamber pots. They watch as* **Arthur** *enters the hall, gags at the smell of the privy, covering his nose with his handkerchief.*)

Bridie Meehan Gagging into his nose-rag, she has him ruinated, he's neither prince nor pauper.

Arthur *Bridie was right. He belonged nowhere except in his mother's over-loving arms and she swept out of their chambers to soothe and mollify him.*

(**Bridie** *and* **Mamie** *scatter as* **Honor** *appears.*)

Honor This is Crothers' rent money. You must take it to him at 49 Stephen's Square. Go, make haste!

Narrator She shut the door on him /

Arthur   *just as she had every time she sent him back to St Eithne's. He'd never felt so low.*

Narrator His jaw throbbed violently /

Arthur   *'Twas like the abiding ache he held for the father he never knew.*

(**Arthur** *retreats.* **Frankie** *enters watching with disgust as* **Ned**, *buckled, enters, collapsing in the street.*)

Frankie *He and Sucky jeered Blubberpuss for havin' no Da but he always wished he hisself had none.*

Narrator Frankie squeezed th'ice blister on his knuckle, the piercing sting lent him some reprieve.

Scene Seventeen: 'Honor Killing'

(*Tosser's Pot.* **Ghost Granny** *and* **Ghost Florrie** *loiter.* **Florrie** *plays aimlessly with the rope of her noose.*)

Narrator   As the murky twilight gave into night down at Tosser's Pot /

Ghost Florrie   There wasn't a soul about.

Ghost Granny   Always dead th'hour after duskfall.

Narrator   Honor lured George Doyle and his *Novelbuke* /

Ghost Florrie   to her oul stretch at th'archway /

Ghost Granny   'twixt Poke's Ally and Cutpurse.

George Doyle (*breathless*)   Let me catch my breath, Honor

Honor   *'Twould all be over in a minute, then she'd give him the slip. He was that befuddled he'd scarce find find his way back* /

Ghost Granny   they always find their way back.

Honor   *She leaned him agin' the wall. He stank of her forgotten mother Florrie* /

Ghost Florrie   strung up /

Ghost Granny   afore the pox putrefied what was left of her.

(**Ghost Florrie** *pulls at the dangling rope, making sounds of asphyxiation.* **Honor** *looks around in panic.*)

Honor   Who's there?

George Doyle   What matter? Touch me, Honor.

Honor   Here, howld your buke for me. // *Her stomach heaved as she reached into his rancid breeches.*

Ghost Granny   On his last legs and still wanting his middle leg fiddled with /

Honor   Did you hear that?

George Doyle (*excited*)   Oh, Honor, whisper your filthy whore's cant to me.

Honor (*gagging*)   *His rancid breath was suffocatin' her* /

Ghost Granny   **put yer shawl-end agin' his coddle box.**

(**Ghost Granny** *lifts up the end of* **Honor**'s *shawl.* **Honor** *places her shawl-end over* **George**'s *mouth.* **Ghost Granny**, **Ghost Florrie** *place their hands on top of* **Honor**'s.)

Honor   *Then she leaned in to George Doyle and whispered the filthiest words a sixth* /

Ghost Florrie   **fifth** /

Ghost Granny   **fourth** /

Honor   *generation streetwalker could summon up from the depths of her sundered soul.*

He was gasping for breath. She tried to lift her hand but it pressed harder agin' his mush /

Ghost Granny   **'til he stiffened and shuddered** /

Honor   *and his ooze seeped out slowly, destroying her glove.*

(**Granny** *and* **Florrie** *release their hands,* **Honor** *follows suit, she is in a trance.*)

Honor   *His body slumped as she moved back. Th'only man who'd ever been inside her* /

Ghost Granny   **slid down the wall**

Ghost Florrie   **His head cracked softly agin' the cobbles** /

Honor   *and Arthur was forever free.*

Ghost Granny/Ghost Florrie   An Honor killing.

Scene Eighteen: 'Circular Insanity'

(*Split scene: Crothers'/O'Rehilly Parade.* **Arthur** *arrives at Crothers'.* **Dorothy** *is chained to the railings.*)

Narrator   Nothing prepared Arthur Gately for the sight of Dorothy Crothers chained to the railings at St Stephen's Square.

Arthur   (*stunned*)   *Her eyes, wild as a tigress, fixed on his before she raised her singular face to the sky, hollering in perfect King's English /*

Dorothy   Votes for Women! /

Arthur   Hear! Hear! /

(**Arthur** *watches, besotted, as* **Dorothy** *easily undoes her chains and drops them to the ground.*)

Dorothy   (*to* **Arthur**)   Well, don't just stand there, pick up my chains and bring them inside.

Narrator   Like all outcasts, Arthur was only waiting on an invitation. He picked up Dorothy's shackles /

Arthur   *and followed her into the gilded world to which he surely belonged.*

(*O'Rehilly Parade.* **Honor** *looks out the window; aggravated by toothache, she rubs her cheek.*)

Narrator   As was her custom, Honor had dressed up the truth that she might more easily live with it.

Honor   (*defensive*)   *She hadn't suicided George Doyle, he'd done it hisself. Was half-dead agin' he got what he asked for. Never paid her neither . . . as was his custom.* (*Pulls tooth out.*)

Frankie   HERALD OR BUGLE! MAN FOUND DEAD IN POKE'S ALLEY!

Narrator   If she'd convinced herself, she was taking no chances all the same.

Frankie   *She asked him to read th'evening edition to her /*

Honor   *gave the sly wretch some stale angel cake.*

Frankie   *He took his sweet time reading about the war in Europe, th'antics of the Rebels /*

Honor   *'til, at last, he got to it.*

Frankie (*reading*)   'Foul play has been ruled out in the case of the man found dead in Poke's Alley. The corpse' /

Honor   That's enough.

Frankie   *He liked looking at her //* Will I read you the funnies?

Honor   No.

Narrator   Months passed. Arthur spent any spare moment away from St Eithne's in the Crothers' mansion.

It was there he realised that his curse was not his paternity /

Arthur   *but his Irishness.* (*Affecting posh.*) *He fell violently in love with Dorothy Crothers and all things English.*

Narrator   Never believing his feelings would be reciprocated, Arthur's tormenters had long ago cemented his belief that /

Arthur   *love would always be one-sided for a colossus such as he.*

(*O'Rehilly Parade.* **Honor** *thrusts a pen and paper at* **Frankie***; he scrawls very fast.*)

Narrator   Ever more desperate to see her son, Honor enlisted Frankie to write on her behalf /

Frankie   *She wanted Blubberpuss to know she was loneful without him and was living only for to see him at the half-term holliers. 'Twas to be sent to /*

Honor   Master Arthur Gately, St Eithne's, Rathrockilly, Co. Dublin.

(**Honor** *ushers* **Frankie** *out the door. Pleased with himself, he tears up the letter.*)

Frankie   *He could read half-decent but he hadn't a nun's notion how to write. Moreover, agin' Blubberpuss didn't come home, happen she'd ask him in again to keep her company.*

(*Crothers' mansion.* **Dorothy** *is having a tantrum.*)

Dorothy (*from off*)   I shan't go ballooning, Uncle. Make Arthur stay here and read to me instead.

Drakewell   *He'd seen one of her eyes dancing askew at breakfast, a sure sign of on oncoming spiral.*

Crothers   Come, Ninian, she's not to be reasoned with. I, for one, will not be denied my amusements.

(*They leave.* **Arthur** *is alone.* **Dorothy** *walks in, clearly manic.*)

Arthur   *No sooner had their carriage departed than she threw open the doors, eyes aflame, wild energy charged the air around her* // I got you a charm for your bracelet.

(**Dorothy** *tosses it aside, circles* **Arthur** *like prey, wrestles him to the floor and straddles him with wild abandon.*)

Arthur   *Ten men twice his girth could not have contained her as she thrust herself upon him. Afore he knew it, she took him inside of her. She was devouring him. He was all she needed and all she wanted. She who was his world. He was floating, above time, free. He thought he would die of bliss . . . Aghhhhhh.*

Narrator   And then it was over.

Scene Nineteen: 'A Dying Wish'

(*O'Rehilly Parade, basement.* **Lil** *is on her deathbed.* **Frankie** *attends her.*)

Narrator   In O'Rehilly Parade Lil Cummins was succumbing to the third biggest killer in the slums /

Mamie Boyle   A mortal dose of the trots, God love her.

Bridie Meehan   And still Ned Cummins couldn't be dug out of the Carter's.

Lil (*gasping*)   Ppp . . . promise me, son . . . . . . never let her have my Ned.

Frankie   Who?

Lil (*with all the bile left in her*)   The hewer.

Frankie   What hewer?

Narrator   Josie Cummins coaxed Frankie away from Lil's corpse.

(**Josie** *puts the scapular around* **Frankie***'s neck. He clutches it tight as she leads him away from the body.*)

Josie   *Gave him her Ma's scapular, afore her Da got hold of it and thrun it away.*

Narrator   Lil's wake was attended by all the tenantry /

(*The* **Players** *enter to form the wake.* **Ned***, sober, shakes hands, etc.*)

Frankie   *except for Honor Gately.*

Ned   *Though she sent down a pig's head and an angel cake.*

Honor   *He'd showed her a kindness once.*

Ned   *Was she thinking as he was?*

Mamie Boyle   Ned, you're no fun unfermented! Go on, take a dram /

Ned   Let me alone, Mamie.

Bridie   I didn't fetch me good blouse out of the pawn for a dry wake.

Narrator   In the three days since Lil's passing Ned hadn't touched a drop /

Ned   *nor had th'inclination to.*

(*The mourners disperse.* **Honor** *listens to* **Mamie** *and* **Bridie** *from the door of her room.*)

Honor   *Lil's month's mind came and went and Ned remained /*

Mamie Boyle   a rechabite. Dry lipped.

Bridie Meehan   Though I hear he's up and down to the privy like a hewer's underthings.

Mamie Boyle   Too late for the kidneys, he'd as well take up the gargle agin'.

Honor   *She'd thought him lost at sea, another reminder of all life had denied her. Then she heard /*

Bridie Meehan   He got work, touting for a knife grinder in Laggard's Lane.

Honor (*rushes to window*)   *Heart a-flutter, she'd watch for him coming back at duskfall.*

Frankie   *His Da spent th'evenings with his head buried in a buke, scarce looking up /*

Narrator   Save when Honor's footsteps moved across the floor above.

(**Ned** *looks up as* **Honor** *crosses the floor.* **Ghost Lil** *hovers behind* **Frankie**.)

Frankie   *The stupefied look on his mush made his Ma's dying words echo inside, the hewer /*

Ghost Lil   *the hewer /*

Frankie   *was Honor Gately*

Narrator   The last soft spot in his broke-up little heart froze hard as ice.

Scene Twenty: 'Sons Undone'

(*Split scene: St Stephen's Square/Meek St.* **Arthur**, *tired and edgy, passes* **Rebels** *as he arrives at the Crothers'.*)

Narrator   Oblivious to the clusters of men armed with sandwiches and rifles moving purposefully about the city streets, Arthur arrived at St Stephen's Square to commence his Easter vigil.

Arthur   *He hadn't been admitted to the Crothers' in the four months since their coupling.*

Narrator   Despite her refusal to see him /

Arthur   *he was consumed with thoughts of Dorothy. For weeks he'd not slept and barely eaten as he languished at the very brink of reason . . . waiting for her.*

Narrator   At last the door of the mansion opened and there she was

(**Dorothy** *appears carrying a rifle.*)

Arthur   My beautiful Dorothy.

Dorothy   And you are precisely who, young man?

Arthur   *She stared at him wildly. One eye dancing askew.*

Dorothy   Out of my way, I am off to partake in the rebellion this morning and this afternoon I'm to marry Ninian Drakewell.

(*The sound of the trapdoor opening echoes.* **Dorothy** *exits leaving* **Arthur**'s *world in ruins.*)

Arthur   *His insides collapsed in a stormburst of agony. The ground beneath him gave way. He was falling off the brink and he couldn't stop himself . . .*

(**Arthur** *backs away.* **Frankie** *enters, pacing up and down.* **Ghost Lil** *in his wake. Distant bullets, windows smashing.*)

Narrator   Frankie Cummins paced up and down Meek Street, willing hisself to do what he must.

Frankie   *All the nights curled up aside the scutterbucket he'd fixed his mind on being all growed-up* /

Narrator   Where Honor Gately would be waiting on him like a stopped clock.

Ghost Lil   The hewer

Frankie   *But now his Da's hatred for her had showed itself as love* /

Narrator   and Frankie knew th'only thing he wanted all his savage little life he'd never get /

Frankie   *Nobody had ever loved him and nobody ever would. He'd made Honor Gately despise him* /

Narrator   because for Frankie, love was a dark and twisted thing.

Frankie   *It was cracked ribs and broken noses, it was wanting and never getting.*

Narrator   'Twas the secrets of others buried within him. And ever since the hewer visited his oozing dreams it was a dark and sticky shame. He crossed over Meek Street /

Frankie (*determined*)   *and done what he came to do.*

Scene Twenty-One: 'Slackvillebine'

(*Slackville St. All* **Players** *form the streetscape. Sounds of sporadic gunfire, windows smashing, discordant sounds: a surreal atmosphere. We are inside* **Arthur**'*s breakdown.* **Arthur** *looks up, awestruck.*)

Narrator   The statue of Nathaniel Carnell stood majestically in the mouth of the street, bullets bouncing off his head as his country announced itself. Yet Slackville Street in rebellion was a wonder to Arthur

Arthur   *The golden hue of blazing fireworks refracted off the shop windows. Ragged strollers and urchins traded shy smiles /*

Ragged Stroller   afore
they smashed the windows /

Urchin   and helped thesserselves to the finery reserved for swanks of th'upper orders.

Arthur   *Factory girls in fancy hats smoked huge cigars. Policemen ran backwards.*

Narrator   Shrieking. Laughter. Howling . . . all tumbled atop one another.

Arthur   *Pearse D'Alton's homemade flag flew atop the post office.*

Narrator   Shots scattered the looters yet Arthur stood spellbound, eyes fixed on a draper's window /

Arthur   *wherein a doleful colossus stared out at him.*

Narrator   He smiled at the poor unfortunate, scarce believing /

Arthur   *that 'twas his own reflection who smiled back.*

Narrator   An undeniable truth dawned on Arthur. He didn't just look like him /

Arthur   *he was Nathaniel Carnell.*

(*A dissonant note sounds above the all the mayhem.*)

Narrator   Gunfire ripped across the street. He felt a tug on his breeches. Feilim Fogarty lay mortally wounded under the statue of Nathaniel Carnell /

D'Alton   *blood spilling from his mouth as he uttered his dying words /*

Feilim Fogarty   Long live Ireland.

Arthur   *Ireland be damned. He would do this the English way.*

Narrator   He took the semi-automatic from Fogarty's already cooling hand.

Arthur (*he aims the gun*)   *He would find Ninian Drakewell and challenge him to a duel* /

Sucky Meehan   Drop your weapon, Blubberpuss!

Narrator   'Twas Bridie Meehan's son, Sucky, newly enlisted to the Empire's army, not expecting his first scalp /

Sucky Meehan   *to be*
Blubberpuss Gately. He'd joined up to excape his Ma, not to die on account of Blubberpuss losing his marbles.

Narrator   Sucky scarpered as Arthur opened fire on the platoon of British soldiers rounding the corner of North Pearl Street /

Arthur   *Drakewells, Drakewells everywhere.* (*He shoots.*) *They dropped like toy soldiers.*

Scene Twenty-Two: 'Confirmation'

(*Split scene: O'Rehilly Parade/Mount-of-Joy.* **Honor** *listens to* **Ned***'s footsteps echo as he approaches.*)

Narrator   Word had gathered apace an uprising was underway /

Honor   *Leaving the tenement so ghostly quiet that she heard each tread of his oncoming step.*

Ned   *His knuckles only hit the wood agin' she flung the door open* /

Honor   *his eyes unclouded by drink, restored* /

Ned   *She'd been rewarded for refusing to accept the life damned to her.*

Honor   *She could see herself in the black of his eye, there was nowhere to hide afore him* /

Ned   *whispering his tendernesses, he leaned into her* /

Honor   *all the world turned soft and warm* /

(**Ned** *kisses* **Honor**. **Peelers** *creep on;* **Frankie** *points them to the door. All are stopped in their tracks by the long kiss, a lifetime in the making. Eventually, one of the* **Peelers** *speaks.*)

Det. Troy   Detective Martin Troy. Honor Gately, you're under arrest. For abortion weaving.

Honor   *His massive carter's hands held her tight to him /*

Frankie   *'til the scaldy-looking Peeler prised them apart.*

Narrator   All the while Frankie Cummins, the sly rat, kept his eyes fixed on Ned.

(*They drag* **Honor** *outside and toward the jail.*)

Narrator   At Mount-of-Joy Jail they left her shivering in the holding cell for hours.

Honor   *All the while his whispered words peacifying her like a lullaby.*

Narrator   The worst had happened and yet Honor was still /

Honor   *Floatin'. Above time. Free . . .*

(*Lights up on the cell as a* **Screw** *pushes* **Honor** *in.*)

Honor   *Then it all went black. A dark night in nowhere.*

(*The sound of the trapdoor, body landing from a height. Over in the house* **Bridie Meehan** *screams.*)

Mamie Boyle   *Poor Bridie Meehan was outside the privy /*

Bridie Meehan   *emptying her chamber pots agin'. Ned Cummins landed just shy of her from five flights up.*

Mamie Boyle (*blessing herself*)   *The Meehans' defecations were strewn all over the corpse.*

(*As* **Frankie** *enters,* **Bridie** *and* **Mamie** *peel back to reveal* **Ned** *dead in the stairwell,* **Ghost Sal** *kissing* **Ned**'s *brow.*)

Narrator   Frankie looked at his broke-up father and for the first time in his life /

Frankie   *he saw a smile on his Da's face.*

Mamie Boyle (*hands him a naggin*)   Here, son, take a sup for the shock.

(*With a flourish,* **Frankie** *throws his head back as he drinks it all in one go: the mirror image of* **Ned***'s first drink.*)

Scene Twenty-Three: 'Love Nation'

Split scene: Kilmayhem Jail/Mount-of-Joy. **Ghost Drakewell** *watches* **D'Alton** *being marched to jail.*)

Narrator   Mere days later, Pearse D'Alton and his militia of boy soldiers were carted off to Kilmayhem Jail. Another failed rebellion /

D'Alton   *yet a glorious failure.*

Ghost Drakewell   Not for Ninian Drakewell, felled by a stray bullet on the way to marry Crothers' insane niece.

Narrator   They flung D'Alton in the cell beside Arthur. Surely the truth would out now.

Arthur (*taps on a pipe*)   Mhaistir D'Alton? It's me, Arthur Gately, tell them I'm no rebel. You know I care nothing for Ireland. My mind came undone, mine was a crime of passion.

D'Alton   No greater passion can there be than to die for love of nation.

Arthur   A nation that exists only in your dreams!

D'Alton   Happen that beyond the dream it already exists, waiting for us.

Narrator   Arthur despaired. He ached not for his phantom father but for Honor.

(*Rattle of the key and sound of cell door opening.*)

Arthur   *He'd thought it would surely be her, to forgive and over-love him at the last.*

(*A* **Priest** *and* **Dorothy** *enter.*)

Dorothy   Arthur, darling. I've come to marry you.

Arthur   *What had he ever seen in her thinly disguised charms?*

Priest   Do you Arthur Florence Gately take Dorothy Ethel Crothers to be your lawful wedded wife?

Dorothy   He does.

Arthur   *He could see the swelling of her belly already.*

Priest   I now pronounce you man and wife.

Arthur   Will you call him George? I don't know why but I always liked that name.

Dorothy   *Of course he would presume the child would be male.* // I must hurry to get the notice in the newspapers before they shoot you. Toodellooo. (*They leave.*)

Arthur   *So this would be his legacy, another fatherless child, likely cursed as he was. D'Alton knew nothing of love, love had melted the borders of his mind and made a murderer of him. Now he was to die all he wanted was to cling on to his cursed life. What nation could be built on love? Out of what would spring his dream? Ireland was /*

Honor   *a virgin, hewered out /*

Frankie (*V.O.*)   *a beaten, hungry child /*

Ned (*V.O.*)   *a love drowned in drink /*

Lil (*V.O.*)   *an unanswered prayer /*

George Doyle (*V.O.*)   *a thousand shameful secrets /*

Multiple Voices Echo (*V.O.*)   *a million hungry ghosts.*

(**Arthur** *fades into the dark. In the playing area tiny red lights appear, the soldiers' fags. English voices.*)

Narrator   The red tips of the soldiers' cigarettes danced like fireflies in the darkness.

Arthur   *Falling quiet when they saw him, they lined up to do their task.*

(*The spotlight appears with crosshairs in in.* **Arthur** *steps into it.*)

Arthur   *He would be first to die. They denied him a final sunrise.*

Narrator   Arthur refused the offer of the blindfold.

Arthur   *He'd always been terrified of the dark.*

(*A hail of bullets.* **Arthur** *falls. A beat of silence.* **Sucky** *is led on by a* **Screw** *and put into the cell.*)

Narrator   'Twas weeks later when Sucky Meehan, AWOL from Empire's army /

Sucky (*buckled*)   was flung into the Mount-of-Joy for drunken affray /

Narrator   that Honor learned of her son's fate. Sucky's ballad floated on the night air . . .

(*Light up on* **Honor** *as she listens to his song, distraught.*)

Sucky Meehan (*singing*)

> Brave Arthur Gately and his
> widow bride,
> The lovers that are Eireann's pride . . .
> Shot at dawn, his bride did cry,
> He looked the cowards in the eye.

End of Act One. Interval.

Act Two

Scene One: 'Freedom-ish'

(Split scene: street/O'Rehilly Parade. Darkness. As the audience return, **Sucky Meehan** *sings.)*

Sucky Meehan *(sings)*

> Two terrible wars in quick succession
> Left the populace in a black-dog
> depression
> Freedom was one thing what to do with
> it another
> What was it to be Irish with brother
> killing brother.
>
> So men in black dresses took over the
> nation
> Preaching penance, prayer and
> self-flagellation
> Everything banned by the censorship
> board
> Except pub-ili-cations in praise of the
> lord
>
> Childer brainwashed by religious
> education
> Trouser pockets sewn up to prevent
> masturbation
> All bodily urges were the work of Oul'
> Nick
> The dreamed-of repub-il-ic was a
> Hierocraship

*(****Sucky*** *dies. A sign 'Emigration Office' points to the basement. The* **Tenantry** *are in their rooms, furtive, backs to the audience. In the front room, two unlit portraits hang, a stack of books nearby.* **Nell Nell** *finishes praying.)*

Narrator   'Twas winter 1950, eighteen years since Nell Nell /

Nell Nell (*turns around*)   *had killed her own mother.*

Narrator   And while her Daddy had forgiven her mortal sin /

Nell Nell (*guilty*)   *he always went to mass alone on that day. Leaving her at home with her catechism.*

Narrator   Nell Nell, grandaughter of patriot hero Arthur Gately /

(*The portrait of* **Arthur Gately** *lights up.*)

Ghost Arthur   knew more about the dangers to her chastity than she did about herself.

(**Nell Nell** *fears she's hearing voices; she takes one of her pills. Outside,* **Cornelius** *enters.*)

Narrator   O'Rehilly Parade was under the landlordship of her father, Cornelius Considine.

Layabout One   As mean a man as ever shat.

Cornelius   The tenantry was made up of respectables now.

Narrator   Tormented batchelors, voluntary celibates and crooked prison officers.

(**Tenantry** *all turn around, as if caught in the act.* **Cornelius** *coughs loudly.* **Nell Nell** *opens her catechism.*)

Narrator   Cornelius had married Arthur and Dorothy's daughter Hibernia Gately /

Cornelius   *Hoping the patriotic connection would seal his bid for leadership of the Greyshirts.*

Narrator   It didn't. Irish fascism failed so he focused his controlling urges on /

Cornelius (*enters front room*)   *his Mary's little lamb. Reared as the ideal of chaste Irish womanhood.* (*Coughs.*)

Nell Nell   Your cough is getting worse, Daddy, would you not go see Doc Slavin?

Cornelius (*ignoring her*)   Did Mr Killbritain drop off his rent?

(**Nell Nell** *shakes her head.* **Cornelius** *sighs, looks indulgently at* **Nell Nell** *and gives her a small jewellery box.*)

Cornelius   I suppose you're waiting on this. Happy birthday! My silly little ninny.

(**Nell Nell** *hugs him; he's stiff, physically uncomfortable. She opens the gift: it's not what she was expecting.*)

Cornelius   Fratelli's rosary beads. The strongest set on the market.

Nell Nell   They're . . . lovely. (*Hesitates.*)   But, Daddy, what /

Cornelius   Ah, ah, now . . . what do questions lead to?

Nell (*resigned*)   More questions.

Cornelius   Never mistake ignorance for stupidity, my little flittergibbet!

Nell Nell (*blurts out*)   But you promised me when I was eighteen you'd give me her wedding ring.

Narrator   The words were hardly out when she wished them in again /

Cornelius (*suddenly furious*)   I never said any such thing. Your mother's ring was buried with her.

Narrator   Hibernia Gately had died giving birth to Nell Nell.

(*A dissonant note sounds.* **Nell Nell** *circles her left wrist in the crook of her right hand – a nervous tic of hers.*)

Nell Nell   *Any talk of her upset him. Why had she opened her stupid mouth!*

Cornelius   You must be having an attack of imaginitis. I don't think those tablets are working at all /

Nell Nell   They are . . . Daddy, I'm sorry. I /

Cornelius   Enough! I've
to get this mountain of filth ready for the Bishop to ban.
(*Takes up some books.*) Go fetch the angel cake, before Fr. Iggy
gets here. And no dilly-dallying, take the cut-through

Nell Nell   But I /

Cornelius   Go! Go!

Scene Two: 'The Saint Weaver'

(*Split scene: street/O'Rehilly Parade.* **Layabouts** *play pitch and
toss.* **Nell Nell** *exits as* **Fr. Iggy Rigney** *enters.*)

Narrator   Fr. Iggy Rigney was born in Tubbercurry St. /

Layabout One   or Tuberculosis St. as it was known local /

Layabout Two   three brothers carried off afore they were
ten years old /

Fr. Iggy   *'Twas that hardened his heart and set him thinking
about getting a vocation.*

Narrator   The country being as it was, a collar was a good
a crown

(**Fr. Iggy** *tosses a coin, inserting himself into their game, then
signals at the* **Layabouts** *to take their turns.*)

Fr. Iggy   *He'd never've made a Jesumenical, there was no
aspiring to that, but neither would he settle for life as a Charitable
Brother.*

Narrator   The Holy Spirited Fathers had seen his potential
to be their 'man on the ground'/

Fr. Iggy (*resentful*)   *keeping dibs on what the Hierarchicals
feared most of all* /

Layabout One   *those with no power /*

Layabout Two   *with nothing to lose /*

Layabout One   *and ripe for conversion by Russia.*

(**Fr. Iggy** *wins and collects the* **Layabouts'** *last few pence.*)

Fr. Iggy   Get yisserselves up to the castle in the morning, lads, there's a bit of work going. Book burning.

Layabout Two   Thanks, Fr. Iggy.

Narrator   But 'twasn't only his lowly origins held him back. Iggy liked to gamble.

Fr. Iggy   *So they had him by the proverbials. But the gamer always has a game-plan. He would deliver up a tenement saint. A saint for and of the poor, to thwart the red menace in the slums and take the boy from Tubbercurry St. to Rome /*

Narrator   where his Dub-bel-lin brogue would melt like incense smoke into th'Italian air.

(*O'Rehilly Parade.* **Fr. Iggy** *heads to the house.* **Cornelius** *opens the door, coughing, ushers him inside.*)

Fr. Iggy   That cough still at you, Cornelius?

Cornelius   It's only a touch of chestitits, Fr. Ig.

Fr. Iggy   *That was a death rattle if ever he heard one. Best get on with it while th'oul pinchfist was still perpendicular* // I told the Bishop that you've the portrait of himself right beside brave Arthur Gately /

Cornelius   Sure didn't you hang it yourself, Fr. (*Coughs.*)

Fr Iggy (*offers his cigarettes*)   Here, take a cigarette to kill th'infection.

Cornelius   Does the Bishop know that cesspit the Empire Theatre is bringing Fancy Cunningham to town?

Iggy   The rabble-rousing Commie hisself. Some set of pipes on him to be fair.

Cornelius   A pure lackey of the Russians! (**Iggy** *lights the cigarette for him*.)

Fr. Iggy   I'm told the Bishop wants the Vatican to make our very own Holy Francis Cummins venerable.

(*The portrait of 32-year-old* **Frankie Cummins** *beside the portrait of* **Arthur** *lights up*.)

Ghost Arthur   Oh please . . .

Ghost Frankie   If you can be a hero, Blubberpuss, I can be a saint.

Fr. Iggy   And his gracious says you're the man can accelerate the path to sainthood. Think, Cornelius, a chapel in the basement where St Francis of the Tenements lived and died in his penitent's chains. Hallowed ground, where the poor can worship and bear witness to his miracles . . .

Cornelius   *He'd lose the rent from th'emigration office*.

Fr. Iggy   *If his fist clenched any tighter he'd draw blood*. (*Turns to the window*.) *But there were no cheap seats in th'eternal kingdom*.

Narrator   Th'air stuck in Cornelius' windpipe, no denying the galloping lurgy now as /

Cornelius (*terrified*)   *pain shot across his chest like electric tentacles* /

Narrator   while Iggy's mind galloped with divine anticipations /

Fr. Iggy   *A rosary at duskfall . . . the suggestible minds of devoted supplicants. . . A brace of miracles was all he needed to get to Rome*.

(**Cornelius** *collapses. Panicked,* **Fr. Iggy** *rushes to his side*.)

Fr. Iggy   *He'd nothing on paper . . .* // Talk to me, Cornelius.

Cornelius   . . . Kill . . . Kill . . .

Fr. Iggy   *Not another civil war confession* // Easy now, God is listening.

Cornelius   Kill . . . Killbritain's rent is overdue, make sure he . . .

(**Cornelius** *croaks.* **Iggy** *takes the cigarette off the floor and leisurely smokes the last of it.*)

Fr. Iggy   *The house'd belong to the nitwit daughter now, he'd have to get to work on her lickety-spit. But sure wasn't a dying wish as good as a golden ticket?*

Scene Three: 'Brain-Rinsed'

(*Split scene: street/O'Rehilly Parade.* **Layabouts** *loiter. We hear the sound of a struggle, a woman hyper-ventilating coming from the cut-through to Tubbercurry St.*)

Narrator   Happen it was the ghost of one language haunting another that left the populace inclined to a curly way of thinking. But the Hierocraship ran in straight lines, all doubt, all confusion had one source:

(**Nell Nell** *emerges from the cut-through with the angel cake, breathless as if she's being pursued.*)

Nell Nell   Satan.

Narrator   The Divil was always on the hunt for Mary's little lambs /

Nell Nell   *making you hear voices that weren't there* /

Narrator   strange echoes in the cut-through, the long-remembered promise of her mother's ring /

Nell Nell   *It was her imaginitis all along. Daddy would never lie!*

Narrator   Imaginitis was the handiwork of the bould Lucifer himself. And if Doc Slavin's pills weren't working /

Nell Nell (*terrified*)   *Daddy would send for a priest to drive it out of her.*

(**Nell Nell** *arrives in the door.* **Cornelius** *is stretched out on the floor.*)

Narrator   Nell Nell worried her way home for nothing. Agin' she arrived back with the angel cake /

Fr. Iggy   *all th'oul' fella was sending for was his wooden overcoat //* He's gone home, my child.

(*The sound of a trapdoor opening echoes.* **Nell Nell** *drops the angel cake, rushes to the body.*)

Nell Nell   No. Daddy . . . Wake up!

Fr. Iggy   *And him dead as a dodo. The innate imbecility of the female condition never failed to irritate him.*

Nell Nell   I killed him with my stupid questions!

Fr. Iggy   *There was no need to disabuse her of the notion. //* He was addled when I got here alright but once he told me his dying wish . . . he smiled as he went home /

Nell Nell   What did he say, Father?

Fr. Iggy   He wanted to build a chapel to Holy Francis Cummins in the basement of this house. A beautiful wish.

Nell Nell (*breaking down*)   Oh, Fr. Iggy, what will I do without him?

Fr. Iggy   You must do as he wished, so his immortal soul can rest in peace. I'll go fetch Doc Slavin. Now, quick, cover up that mirror before his spirit gets trapped inside it.

(**Fr. Iggy** *leaves. Panicked,* **Nell Nell** *goes to cover the mirror; she gasps in horror.*)

Narrator   Nothing prepared Nell Nell for the sight of what she didn't see in the mirror /

Nell Nell   *She had no reflection.*

(*She covers the mirror in panic. Looks tearfully at* **Cornelius**' *corpse, circling her wrist in her hand.*)

Nell Nell   *She was nothing without him.*

Ghost Arthur   unready for life, utterly dependent on him /

Narrator   and Doc Slavin's pink pills /

Ghost Arthur   a Mary's little lamb to the slaughter.

Scene Four: 'Vincent'

(Split scene: Mount-of-Joy/Carter's Arms/docks. **Vincent Meehan** *sings, a* **Screw** *walks him to a cell. Lags mop landings, slop out. At O'Rehilly,* **Ghost Bridie Meehan** *enters with a bundle of belongings, sits on the step.)*

Vincent Meehan (*sings*)

> Oul' Bridie Meehan had a lush for
> a spouse, ten childer she reared in a
> tenement house
> While he gargled the rent, the drunk
> and the louse
> All she had for to pawn was *Hunger's
> Blouse*

Narrator   Vincent Meehan was all talk. Son of th'infamous street singer Sucky Meehan and like his late Da /

Vincent   a frequent inmate of the Mount-of-Joy. During this last stretch he'd spent a hape o' time in solitary /

Screw (*clearing throat*)   **due to an unmentionable** misdemeanour.

Vincent   Given his natural verbosity, th'endless solitude had a detrimental effect on him. Without gargle to soothe his disturbances, he fell victim to th'only diversion available . . . he took up the scribbling /

Screw   and the attitudinising that went along with it.

Narrator   Vincent Meehan plundered the family jewels, his granny's stories, his Da's forgotten songs.
He rehashed jaded oul' street myths in his grandiose vernacular /

Vincent   and in a matter of weeks, he'd produced his very own manuscript. *Hunger's Blouse*.

A tale of life in a Dub-bel-lin tenement in the 1920s and 30s.

(**Screw** *leads* **Vincent** *out of his cell. He struts past the other lags, tucking his manuscript under his arm.*)

Vincent   They couldn't say Vincent Meehan was all talk now . . .

(*The Carter's forms. Lags become* **Locals**, *they sit on one side,* **Hennessy**, **Manly**, **O'Buachalla**, *on the other.*)

Vincent   The Carter's Arms had latterly become the watering hole of several individuals of a literary bent /

Narrator   The Scribbleratti /

Vincent   immediately recognisable by their ridiculous fedora hats /

Narrator   rather than for the novels they were failing to write.

Vincent   U-ni-versity graduates to a man, they sat aside /

Tenement Wetbrain   the hollow-legged communists /

Hollow-Legged Communist   and tenement wetbrains /

Hennessy   touching drinks off visiting American scholars /

Manly   in the thrall of George Doyle's visionary masterpiece *Novelbuke*.

All   The Carter's Arms featured on page 964.

O'Buachalla   They drank off the back of Doyle's genius /

Manly   while crushed by the weight of his legacy.

Vincent (*gleefully*)   For with Dub-bel-lin as their canvass the masterpiece had already been painted.

O'Buachalla   They found succour in lacerating the vastly inferior works of others.

Hennessy   Any halfwit could get their book banned in the Churchstate /

Manly   so the measure of merit couldn't be simply failure /

O'Buachalla   but what, precisely, you were failing for.

Hennessy   The Hierocraship made them hostages to the future /

Manly   success, if it ever came, was for the dead.

Vincent   Vincent Meehan was damned if he was going to settle for a posthumous career in arseless trousers.
There was only one place an Irishman could succeed /

All   Abroad

Narrator   So he snatched up his magpie manuscript and he made for the docks along with /

(*The* **Emigrants** *enter and form a line for the cattle boat.*)

Vincent   Th'excapers, the runaways /

Banished   the banished /

Bewildered   the bewildered /

Vincent   and any soul else as couldn't bear the forbiddance and foreboding of the Hierocraship. They took the cattle boat and knee-deep in puke and porter, they sailed back to th'ould oppressor in search of freedom.

Scene Five: 'The Awakening'

(*Split scene: O'Rehilly Parade/street.* **Ghost Bridie** *sits on the step outside. Inside,* **Nell Nell**, *vacant and dishevelled-looking, as the radio plays.*)

Radio (*V.O.*)   Holy Francis Cummins was born in dire poverty in Dublin in 1900. A reformed alcoholic, he died at the age of 33, his body wrapped in chains. Worshippers gather at his shrine in O'Rehilly Parade where favours are regularly granted. Local supplicant Mabel Tynan claims that /

(**Mabel Tynan** *appears on basement steps, drops to her knees.*)

Mabel   Holy Francis Cummins appeared to me and gave me the cure for Galloping Lurgy. A miracle!

(*Radio sounds fade to a low mumbling rosary.*)

Narrator   Over a month had passed since Cornelius took his dirt nap and Nell Nell remained stupefied /

Nell Nell   *by the lack* *of him.*

Narrator   Time stretched in elastic minutes of endless days. Not a screed of rent had been paid neither. Supplies of everything had run out.

(**Nell Nell** *goes to take a pill but the bottle is empty. Panicked,* **Nell Nell** *holds out her hand, it shakes.*)

Narrator   Without Doc Slavin's pills, Nell Nell's nerve endings were all a-jitter.

Nell Nell   *Her legs felt like lead . . . the room was spinning.*

Ghost Arthur (*worried*)   **Is one of her eyes dancing askew?**

Ghost Frankie   It's the DTs . . . the jimjams . . .

(*Radio sounds fade up again.*)

Radio (*V.O.*)   Fr. Iggy Rigney who leads the miraculous twilight rosaries hopes /

Fr Iggy (*V.O.*)   to travel to Rome with –

(*Radio cuts out and the lights as the electric supply is cut off. The* **Tenantry** *shout from their rooms.*)

Voluntary Celibate   Miss Considine, th'electric is cut off!

Tormented Bachelor (*banging on the door*)   We know you're in there!

Narrator   By duskfall, Nell Nell's hereditary terror of the dark roused her to search for a candle.

Nell Nell   *The only one to be found was the blessed one from Daddy's wake.*

(**Nell Nell** *lights the candle,* **Ghost Cornelius** *appears behind her. She senses a presence but can't see him.*)

Ghost Cornelius   I'll tackle this shower of freeloaders.

Narrator   Nell Nell watched in horror as the door flew open and slammed shut by itself . . .

(**Nell Nell** *hides in the corner.* **Ghost Cornelius** *gets* **Crooked Prison Officer** *in a choke-hold, grabs* **Voluntary Celibate** *by the collar and throws them out. He kicks the* **Tormented Bachelor** *as he scarpers after them.*)

Ghost Bridie   'Twas a sight to behold /

Tormented Batcheor   as the Tenantry
evacuated /

Voluntary Celibate   the bejapurs scarified out of them /

Crooked Prison Officer   be th' invisble agent of Belezebub. (*They exit.*)

Ghost Bridie   Himself stood sentry 'til Killbritain slinked back home in the dark /

Killbritain (*enters, buckled*)   *four sheets to the wind.*

Ghost Cornelius   You're in arrears, Killbritain. (*Brings him down with a fascist salute.*)

Ghost Bridie   Agin' th'oul' shut-purse set about extracting what he'd come back for, she took th'opportunity to slip through th'open door.

Narrator   For the eighth time, habitual evictee Bridie Meehan took up residence in No 1. O'Rehilly Parade.

Ghost Bridie   'Twas good to be back in her rightful.

Narrator   Tuppence ha'penny was all Cornelius retrieved of Killbrittian's arrears.

(**Ghost Cornelius** *enters front room, lifts a floorboard and puts the money in his stash tin.* **Nell Nell** *sobs in the corner.*)

(*She doesn't see where he hides the stash tin.*)

Ghost Cornelius   Hush now, child. Didn't I run the rotten lot of them for you?

(*Seeing her distress.*) **Shhh now . . . my Mary's little lamb. Daddy's here . . .**

(*But it's too late for that.* **Ghost Bridie**, *holding the candle, stands between him and* **Nell Nell**.)

Ghost Bridie   Rightio, back to the boneyard with you /

Ghost Cornelius   But I never got to /

Ghost Bridie   We only get the one wish.

(**Ghost Bridie** *blows out the candle. Darkness.*)

Ghost Bridie   He wasted his, th'oul' tightfist.

Scene Six: 'Iggy's Misfortune'

(*Split scene: outside P.P.'s office/O'Rehilly Parade*)
(**Fr. Iggy** *paces; agitated, jittery.*)

Narrator   Despite the promising start to Fr. Iggy's saint-making, once his Roman dreams took flight /

Fr. Iggy   *He hadn't been able to stop his brain galloping with anticipations.*

Narrator   Nor his hand from dipping into the parish purse.

Fr. Iggy (*bitterly*)   *All Canon Fotrill's racetrack tips were duds!*

Narrator   Lost a fortune at a card school to Al Mostafa. Yet only when confronted by the furious P. P. did he reluctantly /

Fr. Iggy   confess his transgression.

(*A suitcase is pushed on.* **Iggy** *takes looks at it, resentfully.*)

Fr. Iggy   *Th'invisible communists were off the hook /*

Narrator   and Fr. Iggy was assigned the more pressing task /

Fr. Iggy   *of the misfortunates . . .* (*Faint sound of a baby's cry.*) *. . . and their little misfortunes. He'd settled on a vocation for a reason and it wasn't to sort out the messes of weak-willed and mentally deficient girls.*

Narrator   But the Hierarchicals had their caste system and the boy from Tubbercurry Street /

Fr. Iggy   *was an untouchable, one of those with nothing to lose.*

Narrator   There'd be little time for saint-weaving now with all the travelling he'd be undertaking.

Fr. Iggy (*picks up suitcase*)   *He'd best get things in O'Rehilly Parade boxed off afore he left.* (*He exits.*)

(*O'Rehilly Parade.* **Nell Nell** *emerges from the worst of withdrawal.* **Ghost Bridie** *comes downstairs with a chamber pot.*)

Narrator   'Twas two days later when Nell Nell woke from her delirium with an agonising pain in her noggin /

Nell Nell   *and a half-dreamt memory of all hell breaking loose . . . like the house itself had come alive.*

Narrator   Yet all the doors hung open, all the rooms were empty

Ghost Bridie   The tenantry having evacuated thesserselves.

(**Ghost Bridie** *goes into the privy, the door creaking behind her,* **Nell Nell** *comes into the hallway.*)

Nell Nell   Hello? Who's there?

(*The sound of* **Ned**'s *footsteps descending begins, she looks up towards the attic.*)

Nell Nell   Is that you Mr Killbritain?

(**Ned**'s *footsteps get louder passing her as they continue down to the basement. She is terrified.*)

Narrator   Without Doc Slavin's pills, Nell Nell's mind felt crystal clear. For once, she was sure of something /

Nell Nell *she couldn't spend another night under this roof.* (*She exits quickly.*)

Ghost Frankie   Where's she going to go?

Ghost Arthur   England if she has any sense . . .

Narrator   Before his ship set sail, Fr. Iggy Rigney stopped off at O'Rehilly Parade.

(**Fr. Iggy** *enters, whistles to the* **Layabouts***, they follow him down to the basement. He switches on his torch.*)

Narrator   In dark corners of the basement Iggy sought his evidence, scouring it for relics.

(*The* **Layabouts** *and* **Iggy** *pick up objects;* **Iggy** *putting potential relics in his suitcase.*)

Layabout One   A rat-eaten cover of Marxbuke /

Layabout Two   *a length of chain /*

Fr. Iggy (*excited*)   *A scapular /*

Layabout One   a scutterbucket /

Fr. Iggy (*intrigued*)   *A charm bracelet.*

(*He holds it up. Everyone onstage stops for a nano-second. He puts the charm bracelet in the suitcase, closes it.*)

Fr. Iggy   *There was enough here to bypass the P.P. and take straight to Th'archcleric.*

(**Fr. Iggy** *leaves basement, bangs on front door. He tosses the* **Layabouts** *a cigarette for their troubles as he waits.*)

Fr. Iggy   *He wanted to check the chapel paperwork was on track . . . but the nitwit wasn't home.* (*Checks his watch.*) *The P.P.'d given him a prepaid ticket and only enough cash to cover his grub. If he hurried he could make something on a tidy little accumulator before he was took to the ferry.*

Scene Seven: 'The Truth Dawns'

(*Split scene: Solicitor's office/Empire stage door.* **Mr Proudfoot** *sits opposite the dishevelled* **Nell Nell**.)

Narrator   Proudfoot, the solicitor, explained that Cornelius had left Nell Nell nothing.

Nell Nell (*shocked*)   *Not even the haunted house was hers.*

Proudfoot   It belongs to a Mrs Dorothy Crothers-Gately-Le Fanu, your maternal grandmother.

Nell Nell   I have a grandmother?

Proudfoot   Her solicitor in London informs me her whereabouts have been unknown for years.

Nell Nell (*panicked*)   I can't go back to that house.

Proudfoot   Look, stay put for now and live off the rent like your Daddy did /

Nell Nell   but the tenantry have all vanished into thin air!

Proudfoot   *No wonder Cornelius kept a tight rein on her. She wasn't the full complement.*

Nell Nell   How am I supposed to survive?

Proudfoot   You'll have to get yourself a job, young lady. (*He takes out a photo.*) I meant to give this to your Daddy last time I saw him, taken back in the good old Greyshirt days (*Fondly makes fascist salute.*) You'd like to have a photo of you with your parents.

Nell Nell   My Mother died giving birth to me.

(*A dissonant note sounds.* **Proudfoot** *reads the back of the photo.*)

Proudfoot   Mr and Mrs C. Considine and Nell, aged 1. (*Gives it to her.*) Grief can muddle the mind.

Nell Nell (*stunned*)   *There she was, her mother /*

Narrator   holding little Nell Nell /

Nell Nell   *in her arms.*

Narrator   How often she'd been wrenched from childhood slumbers crying out for her /

Nell Nell (*bitterly*)   Daddy blaming her terrors on imaginitis.

Narrator   And how in the frigid silences that followed /

Nell Nell   *She'd wept silently into the night for the want of a mother's embrace /*

Narrator   blamed herself for the lack of it.

Nell Nell   Why would Daddy lie to me?

Proudfoot   Ah, now he must have had his reasons. I'm sure 'twas all for the best. G'luck, now.

Narrator   And with that he abandoned the reeling Nell Nell to the street outside.

(*He exits. A group of* **Girls** *enter passing* **Nell Nell***. They form a line.* **Dilly***, 20, a chatterbox, enters, breathless.*)

Dilly   Jeekers! I didn't think I'd make it, I ran all the way from Fratelli's Rosary Bead factory

Nell Nell   *The girl smelled of something pre-remembered . . . could it be the smell of her mother?*

Dilly   My Da would box the ears off me if he knew I was here but the pay is 14 shillings a week!

Nell Nell   What do you have to do?

Dilly   Just smile wide, kick high and do exactly as you're told.

Narrator   Nell Nell was overqualified.

Dilly   It beats putting nails into the little our lords on the crosses. Imagine, we'd get to see Fancy Cunningham when he plays!

Narrator   The stage door of the Empire Theatre opened, the queue began to move. And with no angry father to account to, Nell Nell /

Nell Nell   (*surprised by herself*)   *did as she pleased and walked straight in.*

Narrator   The doors of her monochrome life slamming shut behind her.

Scene Eight: 'What Is a Tyro?'

(*Split scene: Empire stage/Empire wings/O'Rehilly Parade.* **Nell Nell** *walks into spotlight, blesses herself.*)

Nell Nell   *At first, she thought she'd die of the jitters before going on* /

Narrator   But in the spotlight, 3000 faces looking up at her, the body she'd always had to control /

Nell Nell   *took charge of itself . . . her legs kicking themselves higher and higher! /*

Narrator   expressing what her confused mind couldn't and captivating her audience. Nell Nell was /

Nell Nell   *floating, above time, free . . .*

Narrator   And as the thunderous applause washed over her /

Nell Nell   she felt a belonging.

(*Spotlight down. Empire wings.* **Hi-Kickettes** *mill about.* **Val Mooney**, *stiff and nervous, waits to go on.*)

Narrator   Backstage was another story. Nell Nell had a reputation among the Hi-Kickettes as being /

Marjorie   up herself /

'Cepta   the holy showgirl! /

Val (*sharply*)   Shhh! Quiet.

Dan Dan (*from off*)   And now, Empire favourite, king of the emigration ballad, Mr . . . Valentine . . . Mooney!

(**Val** *goes onstage. Applause, whistles, some boos as* **Dan Dan** *enters the wings, begins wiping his jacket.*)

Dan Dan   Pegging fruit from the sewers, management should do something!

Rita   *Dan Dan said Nell Nell was such a terrific kicker* /

Babs   *he put her centre of the chorus*

Dan Dan (*eye rolls*)   *and the established girls all took the hump.*

Marjorie   Who is she anyway? I don't buy her Mary's little lamb act /

(**Dan Dan** *ignores her, looking out on stage.*)

Dan Dan   Ah look-it! They've destroyed Val's slacks again. (*He hears a giggle.*) I've eyes in the back of my head, Marjorie, don't forget that!

(*He shoos the* **Hi-Kickettes** *off to the dressing room.* **Nell Nell**, *stays, looks out on stage, yawns, exhausted.*)

Narrator   The Hi-Kickettes worked three shows a day, six days a week.

Dan Dan   *And Nell Nell was always at the theatre early.*

Nell Nell   *Anything was better than being alone in the haunted house.*

Dan Dan   *She'd listen in the wings to the quiz before the show, repeating the questions* /

Nell Nell   'What is a tyro?'

Dan Dan   *Never once got an answer right.*

Nell Nell   *There was so much she didn't know . . . like nearly everything the Hi-Kickettes talked of* /

(*Empire dressing room. The* **Hi Kickettes** *jostle in front of the mirrors as they dress for a party.*)

Marjorie (*waves a book in a brown bag*)   banned books /

Rita   handsome fellows /

Babs   Chancers and mickey dazzlers /

'Cepta   they whispered and giggled /

Marjorie (*winking*)   a language of secret signs /

All   mind the step, Babs!

(**Babs** *shrieks, they laugh.* **Nell Nell***, desperate for acceptance, laughs but doesn't know why it's funny.*)

Narrator   Adrift in their conversations, the holy showgirl /

Nell Nell   *was ashamed of her silliness*

(**Marjorie** *puts* **Nell Nell***'s rosary around her neck. The girls primp and preen in the mirrors, blocking out* **Nell Nell***.*)

Nell Nell   *The Hi-Kickettes didn't give two hoots about Satan.*

Babs   They'd strut past the stage-door johnnies /

Rita   off to late night parties in velvet backrooms /

'Cepta   with Momo Al Mustafa the Moslem millionaire! /

Babs   and the local hoi polloi /

Marjorie   The Hi-Kickettes were welcome at every party. (*They leave.*)

Nell Nell   *But they never invited her.*

Marjorie   Hey, Nell Nell? (**Nell Nell** *looks up expectantly.*) Say a rosary for us!

(*Fit of giggles off, the rosary is thrown back on.* **Val Mooney** *appears on the step and picks up her rosary.*)

Val Mooney   Don't mind them Miss Considine.

Nell Nell   No matter what I do I can't make pals with them.

Val Mooney   They're beneath you anyway. (*Gives her the rosary.*)

Nell Nell   *That was exactly the kind of stupid thing Daddy would say* // Thank you, Mr Mooney.

Narrator   He lingered a second or two on the step /

Val Mooney   *before he went to fetch his keys.*

Nell Nell   *Marjorie had left her book behind.*

Narrator   And because Nell Nell didn't know that anger could be stealthy, an action you couldn't explain /

Nell Nell   *she took it. And 'Cepta's cigarette case. If they didn't give two hoots about Satan, why should she?*

(**Nell Nell** *leaves.* **Val** *appears back on the step to find she's gone. He sighs, frustrated.*)

Narrator   It was just shy of a year since Valentine and Irene Mooney's dry wedding night.

(**Irene** *enters. She and* **Val** *stare ahead into the bleak mid-distance as the wedding night, a year earlier, is conjured.*)

Val   *She was naked beneath the nightie. His person was hard /*

Irene   *her stomach a clenched fist.*

Val   *He had to gently force her legs open /*

Irene   *his private part jabbed at her /*

Val   *until he made connection /*

Irene   *She wanted to push him off /*

Val   *a force overtook him.* (*A low growl.*)

Irene   *The full weight of him landed on her.*

Val   *He pulled his person out, it stung like nettles.*

Irene   *So that was it, the Marriage Act.*

Val   *They'd get better at it with practice.*

Narrator   But one year in and the Mooneys' marriage bed was still made of ice and thorns. (**Irene** *exits.*)

Val   *Nell Nell would hardly have reached the bus stop by now, he could motor by and offer her a lift.*

Scene Nine: 'Waiting for Nell Nell'

(*Split scene: O'Rehilly Parade/Carnell St. In O'Rehilly Parade.* **Ghost Frankie** *snores lightly.* **Ghost Bridie**, *bored, wanders about.* **Ghost Arthur** *yawns loudly, waking* **Ghost Frankie**.)

Narrator   With Nell Nell at th'Empire and the tenantry evacuated, O'Rehilly Parade was duller than the boneyard.

Ghost Bridie (*sighs*)   **The dead were nothing without the living.**

(**Ghost Bridie** *takes out a scissors and starts to cut her toenails to* **Ghost Arthur**'s *audible disgust.*)

Ghost Bridie   Just like the Ma, looking down his nose on all and sundry.

Ghost Frankie   No choice, has he? He's stuck up here, like me.

Ghost Arthur   Trapped in false identities. Like the Churchstate, built on lies.

Ghost Frankie   You done well out of it all the same, Blubberpuss, the nation's hero.

Ghost Bridie   Sure your mush is on the ten bob note!

Ghost Arthur (*irritated*)   That's Nathaniel Carnell, not me.

Ghost Bridie   No wonder Hibernia suffered with her nerves, Blubberpuss. You always carping on

Ghost Arthur   My poor, cursed daughter . . . A deranged mother and me imprisoned in a myth

Ghost Frankie   You should be happy to be remembered.

Ghost Arthur   I would be happy to fulfil my wish.

Ghost Frankie   You'd be nobody in England. Sucky Meehan even wove a ballad about you.

Ghost Bridie   Ah, my Sucky, drink was the ruination of him.

Ghost Frankie   Got his thirst off his oul' fella, the same as I done.

Ghost Arthur   Not this sins of the fathers drivel again . . .

(**Nell Nell** *enters to the sound of* **Ned**'s *footsteps descending the stairs; she puts her hands over her ears.*)

(**Nell Nell** *steps on the creaky floorboard as she crosses.*)

Narrator   In th'Empire Nell Nell could forget everything, but the past couldn't be hi-kicked away in the empty, haunted house where /

Nell Nell   *objects moved* (*Sees toenail clippings.*)
Stranger's toenail clippings /

(**Nell Nell** *recoils. Embarrassed,* **Ghost Bridie** *blows them away.*)

Nell Nell   *blew themselves away.*

Narrator   Sleep was a stranger, her mind a-swirl with all
the swallowed questions of her life /

Nell Nell   *nobody who could answer*
them. Nobody to care if she was dead or alive. Fr. Iggy hadn't
shown his face in months, not even when Mabel Tynan died
of Galloping Lurgy /

Ghost Arthur   **Ha! there goes his miracle** /

Ghost Frankie   **he'll find**
another.

Ghost Arthur   **But the truth will set us free Frankie.**

Ghost Frankie   **I'd sooner be idolised.**

Narrator   When the Holy Showgirl looked in the mirror,
nothing stared back at her.

Nell Nell   *Marjorie was right, her whole life was an act, to please*
Daddy so he'd forgive her.

(*She shakes her head, turns away from the mirror. She takes the*
photo of Hibernia out of her pocket.)

Narrator   Hibernia stared helplessly out at her daughter. A
silent character in an untold story.

Nell Nell   *Never mistake ignorance for stupidity he always said.*
He made sure she was both, a dummy who didn't even know what
a tyro was.

Narrator   And because Nell Nell didn't know that anger
could be cold as ice /

Nell Nell   *his silly little ninny . . . ripped her Daddy out*
of the picture.

Narrator   Then, just like when she kicked her legs on the Empire stage /

Nell Nell   *she felt like somebody.*

(**Nell Nell** *takes Marjorie's book,* **'Cepta**'*s cigarettes out of her bag, lights up.* **Ghost Bridie** *sees the book.*)

Ghost Bridie (*flabbergasted*)   ***Hunger's Blouse* by Vincent Meehan.**

Narrator   The magpie Meehan's book had made its way back home.

Scene Ten: 'The Failure of Success'

(*Split scene: Horse and Shamrock/Carter's Arms/Crickleburn/ O'Rehilly Parade. In O'Rehilly Parade.* **Nell Nell** *reads* **Vincent***'s buke avidly,* **Ghost Bridie** *at her shoulder. In London,* **Vincent** *is served by barmaid* **Josie Cummins**.)

Vincent   'Twas Eng-a-land where *Hunger's Blouse* found a measure of success among th'immigrants like oul' Josie Cummins, hungry for reminders of home /

Josie Cummins   *without having to suffer the reality of it.*

Vincent   His buke made Vincent Meehan something of a sensation in the Irish enclaves.

Josie Cummins   *But 'twas his renditions of Sucky's songs that drew people around him like flies.*

Vincent   His English pub-ili-sher advanced him a tidy little sum to write another (*burp*) buke.

Josie Cummins   *The money was swiftly siphoned out of his pockets* /

Vincent (*buckled*)   by the pub-ili-cans of Crickleburn, the imbibing emporia of Archaway /

Narrator   and the bath-houses of Nogo. Before long, Vincent Meehan /

Vincent (*passing out*)   had liquefied his assets.

(*The Carter's.* **O'Buachalla** *enters with the buke in a brown paper bag.*)

Narrator   Copies of *Hunger's Blouse* were smuggled back home. A sniff of good fortune coming to a native son had a unifying effect on the two camps in the Carter's.

Manly   Like dogs to a lamppost /

O'Buachalla   they relieved themselves of their appraisals of the book-shaped item /

Local Soak   pilfered from his granny's spiteful memories /

Hollow-Legged Communist   Sucky's songs de-sung. /

Hennessy   Verbally incontinent tenement cant /

Tenement Wetbrain   I'll . . . I'll. . . . say this . . . He's . . . he's no George Doyle

(*They all whoop. Outside Crickleburn tube station.* **Vincent** *wakes up on the street.*)

Narrator   'Twasn't only the failures that struggled with even a sniff of success /

Vincent (*wincing in pain*)   the wanting of a thing and the getting of it being of two entirely different orders.

Narrator   But even paltry success was perishable unless replicated.

Vincent   His pub-ili-sher was beginning to think Vincent Meehan was all talk.

Narrator   A light fur was forming on his tongue.

Vincent   His hankering innards already demanding purchase. Could you spare a cigarette, padre?

(**Fr. Iggy** *zips across the stage with a* **Misfortunate** *in tow.* **Josie** *enters behind him.*)

Vincent   The skypilot paid him no heed /

Josie Cummins   *that being the way*
of the clergy.

Vincent   He took in the bodies strewn around him /

Josie Cummins   *sons of*
the heroes that gave their lives for freedom /

Vincent   laid ossified under th'archways in puddles of their
own piss. He knew how this would end.

Narrator   There was only one thing for it, to return and
draw from the well of inspiration /

Vincent   Dub-bel-lin. As duplicitous
as a hewer's come-on, where disasters and tragedies eclipsed
one another quick as clouds obscured th'itinerant sun.

Josie Cummins   *He touched her for the boat fare, swore on his*
Granny's blouse /

Vincent   he'd be indentured to the gargle no more.

Josie Cummins (*watches him go*)   *She wouldn't be hedging her*
bets on a Meehan.

Scene Eleven: 'Sorority'

(*Split scene: O'Refilly Parade/Empire. In O'Rehilly* **Nell Nell**, *still*
reading, **Ghost Bridie** *at her shoulder.*)

Narrator   *Hunger's Blouse* was the first book Nell Nell read
of her own free will. It was a revelation.

Nell Nell   *It didn't matter that she couldn't make sense of some of*
the stories /

Ghost Bridie   He'd made a hames of her rememberings.
They were all upside thesserselves.

Nell Nell   *She could hear the tenement house Vincent Meehan*
wrote about all around her!

(**Ned**'s *footsteps echo in the hallway, a chain rattles, a cough, a sigh . . .*)

Nell Nell   *Imagined the sounds she heard in the house were characters from his book.*

Ghost Bridie   Ceased fretting agin' she heard a noise.

Nell Nell   *If she couldn't sleep then she could read all night instead.*

Narrator   Cornelius' mountain of filth and indecency made for a finely curated reading list.

(*Stepping on the creaky floorboard,* **Nell Nell** *gets a book from the pile of banned books to* **Ghost Arthur**'*s delight.*)

Ghost Arthur   Seeing the world through the eyes of others blew the blinkers off her own.

Nell   *There was nobody to stop her from doing what she wanted. And what she wanted most was to learn,* (*her brow furrows*) *to understand.*

Narrator   Bought herself a dictionary.

Nell Nell   *A tyro was a beginner. She was a tyro! A tyro at doing* // whatever she felt like!

Narrator   Imaginitis gave way to instinctivitis.

Nell Nell (*looks at the wall*)   That picture of Holy Francis always sent a shiver right through her.

(*The sonic shiver sounds.*)

Nell Nell   He was a miserable-looking wretch. She'd stick him in the basement for Fr. Iggy.

Ghost Frankie   Not the basement . . . nooooo

Ghost Bridie   Just because she hears, doesn't mean she listens.

Narrator   Like Mary's little lamb before her, the Holy Showgirl vanished. The devil-may-care-dancer was born.

(*During this the portrait of* **Frankie** *is moved down to the basement.* **Nell Nell** *reading as she walks, a new attitude about* *her, makes her way to the Empire. Hi-Kickettes form the Empire dressing room.*)

'Cepta   Nell Nell was late for rehearsals after sleeping in twice in one week! /

Babs   Got the answer right to one of the quiz questions! /

Dan Dan   What is an amanuensis?/

Nell Nell   A person who writes down other people's stories for them. (*Winks, taps her dictionary.*)

Marjorie   Finally, she dropped the drowning kitten act.

Nell Nell   I stole your book, Marjorie . . . *Hunger's Blouse.*

Marjorie   Oh that? Keep it, I couldn't get past the first chapter. Zip me up, would you? Gotta look my best,

Momo's taking me to Stuffy's. Toodeloo.

Narrator   Now Marjorie was busy with Mr Al Mostafa, Nell Nell walked herself into the gap.

Nell Nell   She was centre of the chorus after all.

Rita   Soon they were following Nell Nell to the parties /

'Cepta   Afterwards, she invited them back to her haunted house!

(*O'Rehilly Parade. A squeal of fright as the **Hi-Kickettes** burst in and take over the house. A washing line of stockings, gossamer gold, descends. The portrait of **Frankie** is gone. **Ghost Bridie** is delighted by some action.*)

Rita   They ended up back in O'Rehilly Parade so often /

'Cepta   they moved in!

Babs   Didn't make sense to keep paying for digs /

Nell Nell   when they could stay with her for free!

Rita   I bags this room

'Cepta (*passing* **Ghost Bridie**)   Ughh, what a pong!

Rita   Who blew a windie? (*Laughing.*)

Ghost Bridie   The cheeky rossies.

Narrator   O'Rehilly Parade became a sorority of lipstick and laughter.

Nell Nell   *These girls felt like she did so that /*

Rita   acting the maggot /

Babs   talking and bleeding /

'Cepta   feeling blue . . . and giggling anyway /

Nell Nell   *was as natural as breathing in and out.*

Narrator   Their joyful exuberance not dismissed as /

Val Mooney (*enters from other side*)   *Silliness.*

(*Wings of the Empire.* **Val** *watches the* **Hi-Kickettes** *link arms and cross the stage.* **Nell Nell** *doesn't see him.*)

Nell Nell   What did it matter where she came from? It was where she was going that counted. She'd never known such happiness!

Val   *She was always surrounded by those airheaded doxies now, he couldn't get close to her.*

Marjorie (*arriving late*)   *Batted her eyelashes at everyone but him.*

Val   *Her heels got higher, her sweaters tighter /*

Marjorie   *and Val Mooney couldn't tear his eyes away.* (*Exits.*)

Val   *There were no more lifts home /*

Narrator   nothing to cushion his arrival back to his arctic marriage.

(*On the other side of the stage* **Irene Mooney** *comes on.*)

Irene   *She had to give up her job as a librarian when she married.*

Valentine   *Her sisters said she'd have her hands full soon enough.*

Irene   *Yet each month that passed brought the familiar blood-red despair.*

Valentine   We could adopt?

Narrator   But Irene's war was personal. A woman's body was for making babies and hers /

Irene   *had humiliated her. Again.*
(*They exit.*)

(*A baby crying, faintly.* **Fr. Iggy** *crosses the stage, panicked, moving around in a desperate search.*)

Narrator   Fr. Iggy Rigney was deeper in the loser's enclosure than he'd ever been.

Fr. Iggy   *He'd lost an infant at Cheltenbury racetrack!*

Narrator   Nobody handed in the little misfortune. The couple expecting to take delivery raised hell.

Fr. Iggy   *He was done for. The missions . . . No coming back from there.*

Narrator   Agin' Canon Fottrill saved his skin, arranged a replacement and Iggy submitted to the Canon's retreatment programme

Fr. Iggy   *The Jesumenicals were fierce men for the brain voodoo but it beat real voodoo.*

(*A faint voo-dooish rhythm begins.*)

Scene Twelve: 'The Togethering'

(*The voodoo chanting becomes louder, local, holy, these are protest prayers, a vigil outside the Empire.*)

(*Wings of the Empire.* **Dan Dan**, **Val**, **Hi-Kickettes** *watch from the wings as* **Fancy Cunningham** *rehearses.*)

Fancy (*singing from off*)

> The scabs they fall for the Bosses' lie

> I'll fight for the Union, 'til the day I die.

(**Fancy Cunningham** *enters from the stage.*)

Fancy   I cannot rehearse with that racket!

Narrator   The Empire resisted th'archclerical pressure to cancel the Fancy Cunningham concert.

Dan Dan   *Knights of Temperance and Propriety, Crusaders Against Indecency* /

Narrator   and rabid veterans of the anti-jazz movement laid siege to th'Empire Theatre /

Fancy Cunningham   *Their homely faces contorted in outrage* /

Dan Dan   *as they hollered their hellfire* /

Fancy Cunningham   *against the son of emigrants singing songs of the underdog and the working man.*

(**Fancy** *shakes his head in exasperation, exits to his dressing room.* **Dan Dan** *is embarrassed for Ireland.*)

Dan Dan   Ok, we can't risk getting Mr Cunningham out of the theatre 'til the vigil has dispersed. The after-party will take place in the green room.

Rita   Are we stuck here 'til showtime, Dan Dan?

Dan Dan   Yep. Tea and sambos in the kitchenette.

(**Marjorie**, *about to throw up, leaves suddenly.* **Nell Nell** *starts to go after her.*)

Rita   Leave her, Nell Nell.

Dan Dan   Momo Al Mostafa was in Stuffy's last night /

'Cepta   with Dolly La Touche on his arm /

(*They look at each other, shrug and leave. A suitcase is pushed on.* **Marjorie** *re-enters wiping her mouth.*)

Narrator   There was a high turnover in the chorus line.

Marjorie   *Lipstick and shrugs were poor armour in the harsh light of day. You realised too late you lived on borrowed power. What's easy to see in others isn't so easy to see in yourself.* (*Picks up suitcase.*)

Narrator   And when it came, how sudden the fall.

(*Blackout. A thunderous eruption of applause and feet stamping.*)

(*Wings of the Empire.* **Dan Dan**, **Val**, **Hi-Kickettes**, *breathless and excited as they come offstage.*)

Narrator   The atmosphere was electric in th'Empire. The audience erupting at Fancy Cunningham's rabble-rousing version of Brave Arthur Gately

Val Mooney   *How could he ever sing it again after that rendition? His signature tune*

Dan Dan   Let's head to the green room folks!

Nell Nell   I'll be there in a jiffy, Dan Dan. I want to see if I can find Marjorie.

Dan Dan   Tonight of all nights to miss the show? Women, always flipping disappearing!

Val Mooney   *She paid him no heed as she brushed past, so close he could almost* /

Dan Dan   Chop chop people, the hoi polloi are waiting on yous upstairs. (*They all exit.*)

Scene Thirteen: 'The Age of Consent'

(*Empire dressing room.* **Nell Nell** *arrives in the dressing room.*)

Nell Nell   Marjorie . . .?

Narrator   Marjorie was gone, leaving behind the best of her life and a three-word note /

Nell Nell   *addressed to Nell Nell*? (*Opens and reads.*) 'Mind the Step'?

(**Val** *appears on the step.*)

Nell Nell   Jeepers! Mr Mooney /

Val Mooney   Val. Call me Val.

Nell Nell   *It was giving her the willies the way he was staring at her.* // I'm looking for Marjorie . . .

Val Mooney   *His person was hard as rock* // Let me kiss you.

Nell Nell   Why are you acting like this, Mr Mooney?

Val Mooney   Say my name /

Nell Nell   *Something told her not to* /

Val Mooney   Say it.

Nell Nell (*barely audible*)   Val /

Val Mooney   *a current surged through him, there was no stopping him now.*

Nell Nell   You're married, Mr Mooney.

Narrator   Singing started above in the green room. Nobody would hear if she screamed.

Val Mooney   *She put up no resistance as he drew her lips to his* /

Nell Nell (*blurting out*)   they call you Mind-the-Step-Mooney

Val Mooney   *Something broke inside him then.* (*He backs off.*) *He saw himself through her eyes then* and *the reflection shrunk him down to nothing.*

Narrator   Yet before he left, he managed to summon up the necessary.

Val Mooney   It was me told Dan Dan to put you centre of the chorus.

Nell Nell   *And, with that, he ripped away the one true thing she'd built herself around.*

Narrator   The second split in two. Her fragile shell shattered /

Nell Nell/Narrator   she saw herself as others did /

Nell Nell   *a pathetic, stupid, little ninny.*

Narrator   Then she understood Marjorie's three-word warning.

Nell Nell   *A man had the power to make or break a woman for no reason but one of his own choosing.*

Narrator   Turn a somebody back into a nobody.

Nell Nell   *How could she protect herself against that?*

Narrator   The devil-may-care-dancer died quick as one minute falling into the next.

Scene Fourteen: 'The Green Room'

(*Split scene: Empire green room/stage door.* **Vincent Meehan** *sings the end of* Hunger's Blouse.)

Vincent (*singing*)   *All she had for to pawn was* Hunger's Blouse.

Narrator   Three months on the wagon and all spruced up, Vincent Meehan looked almost handsome . . . in a round about sort of a way.

Fancy Cunningham   Comrade Meehan, please, another song.

Narrator   Desperate as Vincent was for the approval of others, when he got it /

Vincent   *it was for Sucky's songs. And, sober, this had a repulsing effect on him.*

Narrator   Flashes of his childhood ran riot across his mind, giving rise to a violent thirst.

Vincent   *His innards hankered. He'd best get out.*

All   Ah, Vincent! / Sure the party's only starting / The harp polishers are still outside / Don't forget your buke . . .

(*Someone shoves his copy of* Novelbuke *into his hand.* **Nell Nell** *appears in the doorway, shaken.*)

Narrator   Nothing prepared the still trembling Nell Nell for the sight of /

Nell Nell (*awestruck*)   *Vincent Meehan /*

Vincent   *The doxie stood in the doorway mouth agape, like an ornamental fly catcher /*

Nell Nell   *Here he was, made human, the man who'd changed everything for her /*

Vincent   *If she didn't stand aside he'd push her into next week*

Nell Nell   *She could see her reflection in the black of his eye.*

Narrator   And Nell Nell sparkled with such admiration that Vincent Meehan's /

Vincent (*surprised*)   *galloping panic relaxified itself.*

Nell Nell   *He leaned in so close she could feel the heat of his breath on her neck /*

Narrator (*knowing*)   And in that moment she knew that it was him /

Nell Nell   *and only him, who could protect her.*

Vincent   Would be so good as to show me th'excape route, miss?

Nell Nell   Follow me, Mr Meehan.

Vincent   Vincent. // *She was that obliging, 'twould've been criminal not to touch her for a few bob* /

Nell Nell   *swore on his granny's blouse he'd be back to repay her tomorrow.*

Vincent   *Gave her his copy of* Novelbuke *as collateral then got hisself swiftly out of harm's web*

(**Vincent** *leaves. The door slams shut.* **Nell Nell** *clutches the copy of* Novelbuke *to her chest.*)

Nell Nell   *She could feel Vincent Meehan still standing there as if no door had slammed in her face.*

Narrator   And because Nell Nell didn't know that fear could enchant and bewitch, she let herself /

Nell Nell   *be swept away like confetti on th'upswell of a warm summer wind.*

Scene Fifteen: 'Three Long Years'

(*Split scene: O'Rehilly Parade/cattle boat/Mooney's. Sounds of destruction. In the front room,* **Arthur***'s portrait has its face punched in. A typewriter lies on the floor, flowers strewn.* **Nell Nell** *enters, tidies up. Outside, the* **Layabouts** *loiter,* **Ghost Bridie** *sits on the step. Emigrants queue for the* (*cattle boat.*)

Narrator   By 1955 the Hierocraship was in economic paralysis. An overall sadness had took hold of the citizenry.

Layout Two   Highest emigration since the Great Starvation.

Layout One   One person left every five minutes.

(**Ghost Arthur** *joins the emigration queue.*)

Ghost Bridie   **Even the dead were abandoning the living.**

Ghost Arthur   **When a chance came, you had to take it.**

**Ghost Bridie   'Twas Vincent set Blubberpuss free
hollering up and down the parade** /

Ghost Arthur   that Brave Arthur Gately was no hero /

Vincent (*roaring from off*)   he
was nothing but a cake-fed, parlour boy!

(*Holding the flowers in her hand, plaster dust from the ceiling falls
like confetti on* **Nell Nell***: a loser bride.*)

Narrator   As the third year of Nell Nell Meehan's marriage
limped on, she was a shadow of herself.

Ghost Bridie   The tenement was silent to her . . . (*Shakes
her head.*)   **All she heard was Vincent.**

Nell Nell   *They'd been married two months when the Carter's
sucked him in.*

(**Nell Nell** *picks up the typewriter and puts it on the table.*)

Narrator   It was a one-sided love. He gave her the
typewriter as a wedding present.

Nell Nell (*defensive*)   *She taught herself to type a 100 words a
minute.*

(*The typewriter starts typing rapidly by itself.* **Nell Nell***, oblivious
to it, collects balled-up papers from the floor.*)

Narrator   The hereditary nimble fingers, however, were
little use in the bedroom

Nell Nell   *She put the wedding night down to nerves.*

Narrator   Excuses piled up like unpaid bills. Ashamed of
his own desires, he warped hers.

(**Vincent** *storms out of the privy, shouting at the top of his voice as
he passes the front room and exits.*)

Vincent   Kicking your legs in th'air, flashing yer rasher for
all to see. No man could want what's given away so easy.

(*The typewriter stops typing.*)

Narrator   Three years in and Mrs Vincent Meehan was still Virginum Integrum.

(*During the following,* **Nell Nell** *opens the balled-up papers, starts to type* **Vincent***'s illegible scribblings.*)

(*The Mooneys' sitting room.* **Val** *brings on a TV set, fiddles with the rabbit's ears.* **Irene** *watches.*)

Narrator   As the Hierocraship tightened its grip, change could only come from without.

Val Mooney   *There were fifty new TV sets being sold per week.*

Narrator   Fallout signals from British channels could be picked up along th'east coast of the Churchstate.

Val Mooney   *He'd bought one outright using their holiday money. There was no need to put them through the torture of a rainy fortnight in Golden Strand with her ever-pregnant sisters.* (*Takes her hand.*)

British TV Voiceover   Welcome to *The Whole Wide World Today.*

Narrator   Through a blizzard-like signal British TV took the Mooneys beyond the Hierocraship to a world where there were other ways to be.

Vincent (*shouting from off*)   Nellser! Nellser!

(*O'Rehilly Parade.* **Nell Nell** *types,* **Vincent** *enters with the* **Scribbleratti** *in tow, they are all buckled.*)

Narrator   Vincent had long since installed the Scribbleratti in the rooms vacated by the Hi-Kickettes.

Hennessy   *They'd to put up with Meehan's schizoid rants /*

Manly   *but a free place to doss /*

O'Buachalla   *with a resident typist /*

Hennessy   *couldn't be sniffed at.*

Manly   I propose a toast to our delightful, young
amanuensis.

Vincent   Aman-u-whatsits?

Nell Nell   Amanuensis . . . it's a person who writes down
other people's stories for them

(**Vincent** *snorts a mean laugh. He snatches up the un-balled bits of
paper, reads them.* **Nell Nell** *looks nervous.*)

Hennessy   *She measured her responses* /

Manly   *by the curl of his lip* /

O'Buachalla   *or the shade of his temper.*

Narrator   Because love for Nell Nell was a heart-thumping
panic /

Nell Nell   *an unbearable silence*

Narrator   The longing to be held. It was pleasing the beloved /

Nell Nell   *so they wouldn't take their love away.*

Narrator   But there could be no pleasing Vincent Meehan
who continued to find himself disinspired /

O'Buachalla   *his second 'Buke'*
remained unwritten /

Ghost Bridie   He'd used up all her tenement tales.

Manly   *The one story he could truthfully tell* /

Vincent   *was the very one he*
spent his life trying to excape from.

(**Vincent** *rips the page from the typewriter, clears the table in
a rage. The* **Scribbleratti** *leave,* **Nell Nell** *goes to calm him,*
Vincent *pushes her away, she lands on the floor. He leaves.*)

Narrator   In the story of Nell Nell and Vincent, her
unlived life could only get better if he did /

Ghost Bridie   **Marriage was**
forever . . . she'd made her bed and lie in it she must.

Scene Sixteen: 'The Last Days of Empire'

(*Wings of the Empire. Sounds of the unruly audience,* **Dan Dan**,
Hi-Kickettes, **Val** *look out, nervously.*)

Narrator   At the Empire Theatre times were changing.
The unruly element had increased /

Dan Dan   Gougers with
Hollywood hairstyles and velvet collars running amok.

Babs   Since Nell Nell lost her sparkle /

'Cepta   Dan Dan shifted her
from the centre of the chorus /

Babs   down to the last spot . . . near the wings /

'Cepta   where she wouldn't be missed when she didn't
show up.

(*They all look toward* **Nell Nell** *as she enters, her arm in a sling.
Everyone looks awkward.* **Dan Dan** *sighs.*)

Nell Nell   I'm such a ninny. I slipped /

Dan Dan (*taking her aside*)   Look . . . I'm sorry,
Nell Nell /

Nell Nell   No, please Dan Dan . . . I can still kick!

Dan Dan   I have management to answer to.

Nell Nell   The Empire is my family. It's the only place I've
ever belonged.

Dan Dan (*hands her an envelope*)   There's a week's extra in
there, me and the girls had a whip round.

(*The* **Hi-Kickettes** *and* **Dan Dan** *all turn away and busy
themselves.* **Val** *watches her go, smug.*)

Nell Nell   Always the last to know. The story of my life.

(**Nell Nell** *leaves, the Empire door shuts behind her, its
echo reverberating.*)

Narrator   The stage door of the empire shut behind Nell Nell and /

Nell Nell   *the last scrap of the little life she'd made for herself, of who she'd been for that short and happy time before Vincent . . . was gone.*

Narrator   And with it, Vincent's drink ticket. Making her way back to O'Rehilly Parade, Nell Nell realised /

Nell Nell   *She was more afraid of the living than she was of the dead.*

Scene Seventeen: 'Iggy's Golden Ticket'

(*The Archcleric's palace.* **Th'archcleric** *paces.*)

Narrator   The Easter collections were down by 20 per cent. Th'archcleric knew exactly what was to blame /

Th'archcleric   *Cross-channel filth and foreign habits being beamed into Irish living rooms!*

Narrator   And there was nothing he could do to stop it

Th'archcleric   *Canon Fottrill suggested this 'Forward Thinker' . . . in the absence of any better ideas . . .*

(**Fr. Iggy** *enters with his suitcase, kisses* **Th'archcleric**'s *ring.*)

Narrator   Cured of his galloping anticipations, the boy from Tubbercurry Street had spent the last three years /

Fr. Iggy   *Ministering to inebriate immigrants in the doss houses of Crickleburn /*

Narrator   and watching British TV.

Fr. Iggy   They're renting them over there. Hordes of them watching together, one TV set can infect a whole street. Advertisements every few minutes, bombarding the poor with all they can't afford.

Th'archcleric   Exactly what the red menace need to stir up trouble. How can we protect our faithful?

Fr. Iggy   We give them something that costs nothing, a Dublin saint, for and of the poor.

Narrator   And then he fetched her in; his miracle bearer.

Fr. Iggy   *Found her by divine accident behind the bar of the Horse and Shamrock in Crickleburn.*

(**Fr. Iggy** *ushers* **Josie Cummins** *in. She nods, without deference, to* **Th'archcleric**.)

Fr. Iggy   Josie Cummins, your gracious, sole surviving sister of Holy Francis Cummins.

Josie Cummins   *He'd paid her fare. 'Twould be her first and last visit home.*

Fr. Iggy   Miss Cummins is most anxious that we bear witness to what she has to say, your Gracious.

Josie Cummins   I have always wanted the truth known about my brother.

Th'archcleric   Wasn't it Jesus himself who said 'Only the truth shall set you free'?

Scene Eighteen, Doyleseve

(*Split scene: the Carter's Arms/Tosser's Pot/O'Rehilly Parade. The* **Scribbleratti** *wait outside the Carter's*.)

Narrator   The Meehan family history was repeating itself in the Carter's where Vincent was stretching the bounds of obstreperosity /

Manly   and spooking away their American benefactors.

(**Two American Scholars** *enter with a camera. They hover at a distance before the* **Scribbleratti** *pounce on them*.)

Hollow-Legged Communist   Forcing the workshy scribes to come up with a shakedown /

Hennessy   Doyleseve!

Manly   For a healthy fee they steered the visiting yanks away from the Carter's, on a night creep /

(*The* **Scribbleratti** *pursue the* **American Scholars***, charming them as they lead the way.*)

Hennessy   to the nearby locations in George Doyle's *Novelbuke* /

Manly   rambling down O'Rehilly Parade /

Hennessy   quoting passages from the Doylesean masterpiece /

Manly   en route to Tosser's Pot.

O'Buachalla   Ending with a recitation from the final chapter 'Solicitous Honoré'

(*Tosser's Pot.* **Ghost Granny** *and* **Ghost Florrie** *emerge from the archway.*)

Ghost Granny   **Hewering always popular** /

Ghost Florrie   **with them that wasn't hewers.**

Narrrator   As was the yank custom of extending gratuities, the Scribbleratti /

O'Buachalla   were only too happy to pose for a flash photograph /

Manly   when who should stumble out from under the archway /

Hennessy   with a sailor boy?

(**Vincent Meehan** *and the* **Sailor Boy** *emerge just as the flash goes off. The* **Scribbleratti** *are dumbstruck.*)

Ghost Granny   **The mushes on them, like they'd never in their lives seen a Mollie** /

Ghost Florrie   **nor his pink.**

(**Vincent** *pushes away the* **Sailor Boy**. **Ghost Granny, Ghost Florrie** *and* **Sailor Boy** *disappear under the archway.*)

Narrator   While art was a faith, not an occupation, not everyone was a believer. Vincent Meehan wreaked his vagrant revenge in O'Rehilly Parade.

(**Vincent** *watches as pages drop down from above like rain on the* **Scribbleratti***: their posthumous careers ruined.*)

O'Buachalla   Years of words, drafted in icy, sleepless dawns /

Hennessy   the truth that could only be found in fiction /

Manly   warnings to the future of how the past could be betrayed /

Hennessy   swept away on a merciless Dublin wind /

O'Buachalla   A life's work. Squandered.

(**Vincent** *leaves.*)

Narrator   There was nothing for it but the Carter's, where /

(*The Carter's forms around them, the two camps become one. Outside,* **Nell Nell** *enters, picks up bits of paper.*)

Local Soak   despite their airs and graces they were welcome.

Tenement Wetbrain   They believed in something bigger than themselves /

Hollow-Legged Communist   the Scribbleratti were outsiders too /

Local Soak   even if they were well got.

Hennessy   Tomorrow they would start again /

Manly   the doing being as important as the done.

Scene Nineteen: 'The Reflection'

(*O'Rehilly Parade.* **Ghost Bridie** *aimlessly practises on the typewriter.* **Nell Nell** *enters with sodden scraps of paper, stands*

on the creaky floorboard. In the basement, **Frankie Cummins'**
portrait is askew.)

Narrator   The amanuensis salvaged what she could. The
house itself looked like a crime scene /

Nell Nell   *and so ghostly quiet she*
could hear each tread of the oncoming steps.

(**Ned Cummins'** *footsteps begin.*)

**Ghost Bridie   The bottle of liquor on the table had only a
sup gone out of it.**

Nell Nell (*fearfully*)   Vincent?

Narrator   But 'twasn't him, 'twas only a ghost.

**Ghost Bridie   He'd left a message scrawled on the mirror
with her lip paint.**

(*As if she's hearing* **Ghost Bridie,** **Nell Nell** *walks to the mirror.*)

Vincent (*V.O.*)   Gone for good. Forget me.

Nell Nell   *She was twenty-two years old. No one else could marry*
her now.

Narrator   The abiding ache below all the others, deeper
than Daddy's lie, surfaced . . .

Nell Nell   *She hadn't killed her mother /*

Narrator   but Hibernia Gately
had /

Nell Nell   *abandoned her.*

Narrator   The arms that held her had let her go.

Nell Nell   *Nobody had ever loved her . . . and now nobody*
ever could.

Narrator   And in that moment the secrets of strangers
lurking within her demanded their say /

(*With the same flourish as* **Ned** *and* **Frankie,** **Nell Nell** *takes the*
whiskey, drinks: the mirror image of them.)

Narrator   The untold story was Nell Nell's story too.

(**Ghost Bridie** *is unsettled by this.* **Nell Nell** *looks in the mirror.*)

Narrator   For the first time since Cornelius died, Nell Nell saw a faint reflection.

(*The sonic shiver sounds.* **Ghost Bridie** *looks, she gasps.*)

Ghost Bridie Babe of Bethlehem! (*She blesses herself.*) **She looked like the miserable wretch.**

(*In the basement. The frame of* **Frankie***'s portrait in the basement falls apart.* **Nell Nell** *takes another swig.*)

Ghost Frankie   Damn you, Bridie Meehan! I don't want to be free.

(**Nell Nell** *hears the frame crashing to the floor. Loudly,* **Ned***'s footsteps descend to the basement.*)

Ghost Bridie   She listened. And then she followed.

Narrator   If the living couldn't tell her, 'twould have to be the dead.

(**Nell Nell** *leaves, taking the whiskey with her.* **Ghost Bridie** *goes to the typewriter, types with purpose. In the basement.* **Ghost Frankie***, triggered by the sound of* **Ned***'s footsteps, hides in the corner.*)

Scene Twenty: 'Hibernia's Bracelet'

(*Split scene: Archcleric's palace/O'Rehilly Parade, basement. The action is congruent in both locations.*)

Narrator   Josie Cummins bided her sweet time, putting the unflappable Iggy Rigney on edge.

Fr. Iggy   *Not just because she was a female, she had no deference about her. Infected by England.*

(*O'Rehilly Parade, basement.* **Nell Nell** *enters, repeating the* **Cummins***' drinking flourish.*)

Josie   There's a weakness for drink runs through my family. My father, Frankie, one drink was all it took . . .

Fr. Iggy   This was before Holy Francis took the pledge and lived a life of self-flagellation and prayer.

(*O'Rehilly Parade, basement.* **Nell Nell** *picks up one of the chains attached to the wall.*)

Fr. Iggy   These items were found in the basement where St Francis lived and died.

Th'archcleric   And do you recognise any of the relics Fr. Iggy has gathered?

Josie   This was my mother's scapular, Frankie never took it off.

(**Th'archcleric** *nods approvingly at* **Fr. Iggy**. **Josie** *jolted out of her indifference.*)

Josie   Where did you find this charm bracelet?

Fr. Iggy   In a corner of the basement. Do you recognise it? (*Josie nods.*)

(*O'Rehilly basement.* **Nell Nell** *circles her wrist with her hand, then takes a large gulp of whiskey.*)

Th'archcleric   Both you and Holy Francis lived in No. 1 O'Rehilly Parade at the time?

Josie   Yes. I was Miss Dorothy's skivvy. Her daughter, Hibernia suffered with her nerves, swore her dead father's portrait spoke to her. People came to Frankie for cures . . .

(*O'Rehilly basement.* **Nell Nell** *sees the broken frame of* **Frankie**'*s portrait.*)

Th'archcleric   And did Holy Francis cure her of her affliction?

Josie   He couldn't even cure hisself. He'd still lash out on the drink betimes

Fr. Iggy   A patron saint for those cursed by the fondness for cyclical drinking.

Th'archcleric (*nodding*)   The scourge of the slums.

Josie   I warned Dorothy not to let Hibernia near Frankie but she was in one of her spirals.

(*O'Rehilly basement.* **Nell Nell** *passes out on the basement floor.* **Ghost Frankie***, emerges from the shadows.*)

Josie   It was me found her, hysterical on the basement steps, her dress tore open. Her bracelet was missing.

Fr. Iggy   Given as alms, perhaps.

(*O'Rehilly basement.* **Ghost Frankie** *kneels over the prone* **Nell Nell***, wanting but afraid to touch her.*)

Th'archcleric   And she was cured of her nerves, the voices and such?

Josie   Hibernia scarce spoke after that day. She was five months gone before anyone noticed that Frankie, your Holy Francis, had interfered with her.

(*O'Rehilly basement. Dissonant note sounds.* **Ghost Frankie** *starts whimpering pathetically.*)

Ghost Frankie   I'm sorry . . .

Fr. Iggy   This is preposterous!

Th'archcleric   Where is this Hibernia woman now . . . or her mother?

Josie (*shrugs*)   Dorothy Gately married Hibernia off to the Greyshirt Considine and left the country. I was living in London by then. Frankie was found dead a few months later.

(*O'Rehilly basement.* **Ghost Frankie***, softer than we've ever seen him, touches* **Nell Nell***'s brow.*)

Ghost Frankie   I would have loved you . . . my own lovely girl.

(**Nell Nell** *swats him away.* **Ghost Frankie** *takes the whiskey, disappears into shadows.*)

Josie   The tormented turned tormentor. That was my brother.

Fr. Iggy   I think Th'archcleric has heard quite enough of your scurrilous allegations, Miss Cummins.

Josie   Before I go, your Gracious, tell me how the truth would set Frankie's child free?

Scene Twenty-One: 'Valentine's Day'

(*O'Rehilly Parade, basement. A bottle rolls across the floor.* **Val Mooney** *finds* **Nell Nell** *lying on the floor.*)

Narrator   It was Val Mooney found Nell Nell collapsed on the floor of the basement.

Val Mooney   *Reeking of drink, her blouse wide open . . .*

Nell Nell   Mr Mooney . . . what are you doing here?

Val Mooney   It's the last night of the Empire. All the Hi-Kickettes from down the years came to rehearse today. Dan Dan was worried when there was no sign of you. Let me help you up . . .

Nell Nell (*giggling*)   I broke my pledge. (*Sees* **Val** *looking at her open blouse.*) Look at you! Looking at me.

Val Mooney   Stop it. Please.

Nell Nell   Vincent's left me. Never coming back.

Val Mooney   I should leave.

Nell Nell   Then go, go, whydon'tya?

Val Mooney   *The vague burr of a Dublin accent in her inebriation, a pathetic echo of Meehan. It disgusted him what she'd done to herself for that wastrel. And yet . . .*

Nell Nell (*she takes off her blouse*)   He never once looked at me like you do.

Val Mooney   It's hard not to look . . . You're beautiful.

Nell Nell   Couldn't bring himself to touch me. You could still be my first. (*Places his hand on her breast.*)

Val Mooney   Don't . . .

Nell Nell   Stop me then . . . Val.

Val Mooney   I can't, I can't.

(*As the lights dim down, a mist begins to fill the stage.*)

Scene Twenty-Two: 'The Untold'

(*Playing area.* **Josie** *walks on. A* **Misfortunate** *follows. Other* **Players** *drift in and out of the mist with suitcases.*)

Narrator   Josie had an hour to kill before the cattle boat.

Josie   *How these streets had haunted all her English days. The ghosts alive, the living good as dead.*

Misfortunate   A place where fathers disowned their daughters on the word of a priest /

Josie   *then stewed in the silence of swallowed words, lowering their jars into them* /

Misfortunate   Betimes sat beside the man who'd wronged their girl and bought him a ball of malt.

Josie   *There was no belonging here. She belonged to a migrant people* /

Misfortunate   thousands upon thousands of them, banished /

Josie   *to the vice-filled streets of English cities where they had finally learned to breathe. What would happen to the secrets left behind, to all the truths that had sailed away?*

O'Buachalla   There was no resolution /

Manly   no ending /

Hennessy   endings
were what stories were for.

(*The* **Players** *retreat into the mist.* **Josie** *stops outside the house. Inside, the typewriter is going full tilt on its own.*)

Narrator   Josie stopped short outside O'Rehilly Parade.

Josie   *She'd slipped the charm bracelet in her pocket afore she left.*

Narrator   Placed it atop the basement steps.

Josie   *For Hibernia . . . whatever had become of her. Frankie had long ago met his maker.*

(*1932.* **Frankie Cummins** *emerges from the mist, falls to his knees to pray. Takes up his chains.*)

Narrator   'Twas winter 1932 when Honor Gately died in her prison cell. Her corpse still warm

Ghost Honor (*V.O.*)   **agin' she used her wish to the wise.**

(*Another chain loops around* **Frankie***'s neck; he struggles as he is pulled back into the shadows.*)

Ghost Honor (*V.O.*)   **Trussed up the malignant little Judas in his chains.**

Narrator   Stuck a rat in his mouth and left him to rot.

Ghost Honor (*V.O.*)   **For Ned. For revengeance.**

Narrator   Josie turned out of the Parade for the last time.

Josie Cummins   A peace descended on her. She had done her reckoning.

Narrator   Already Dublin was sitting hard on her chest. She cleared her throat. And then she disappeared into the pea-souper of a fog that had engulfed the city.

(A spotlight. **Val Mooney** *steps into it and sings. During this,* **Nell Nell** *crawls up the basement steps, an echo of Hibernia, distraught and bewildered. She finds the charm bracelet, she puts it on her left wrist.)*

Val   Brave Arthur Gately and his widow bride . . . The lovers that are Eireann's pride . . .

Shot at dawn, his bride did cry . . . He looked the cowards in the eye.

Narrator   That night the curtain fell for the last time on the Empire Theatre. Television was coming.

End of Act Two. Interval.

Act Three

Scene One: 'The State of You'

(*O'Rehilly Parade basement/street/front room. Darkness. A siren. Lights up.* **Tiernan** *plays loud, punky guitar as* **Ferdia** *sings.* **Tiernan**'s *hair is spiked, he wears bottle-end glasses and badly homemade bondage trousers.*)

Ferdia (*singing*)

> Brave Arthur Gately didn't die for this
> Politicians praying, priests on the piss
> No rubber johnnies, no abortions
> Not enough chips in Gino's portions

Tiernan (*joins in*)

> Ireland, Liarland, Ireland, Liarland.
> Ireland, Liarland

(**Ferdia** *stops singing and pulls the plug out of the amp.*)

Ferdia   Fuck this . . . I'm leaving.

Narrator   It was summer 1981 when The Bastard Meehans broke up.

(*The sound of the trapdoor opening.* **Tiernan** *is stunned,* **Ferdia** *looks guilty.*)

Tiernan (*talks with a lisp*)   What about the Battle of the Bands? The flyers are printed, Ferdia!

Ferdia   I won't be here. I'm leaving leaving.

Tiernan   Where are you going?

Ferdia   New York.

Narrator   Tiernan waited for his invitation. It didn't arrive.

Tiernan (*furious*)   Have you been planning this all along, while we were making the demo tape?

Ferdia   I knew you'd freak out.

Tiernan   Where'd you get the money?

Ferdia   *And for reasons unbe-fucken-knownst to him, he smiled before he said it //* Dad.

(**Tiernan** *storms out.* **Ferdia** *strums a bum note on the guitar.* **Tiernan** *climbs the basement steps in a strop.*)

(*Street. The chains of his bondage trousers trip* **Tiernan** *up.* **Ghost Mamie Boyle** *enters.* **Ghost Bridie** *smokes her pipe on the steps. They watch* **Tiernan**.)

Narrator   The Meehan twins had never been parted /

Ghost Mamie Boyle   since Ferdia slipped out as the bells rang in the New Year. A huge boy, God bless him. Th'other twin was born hard, in his caul, looked like a little rat.

Narrator   Tiernan Meehan was the loser in the genetic lottery.

Ghost Mamie   Sure one poor scrap could get it all, the rabbit lip /

Ghost Bridie   the gimpy kidney, the bad blood of both sides.

(**Tiernan** *tries to calm himself down.* **Ghost Mamie** *exits to the diddy parlour.* **Ghost Bridie** *yawns.*)

(*Front room.* **Nell Nell***, 47, hippy-ish enters, wearing the charm bracelet and carrying some manuscripts.*)

(*She glances in the mirror and smiles, comfortable with her reflection, a different person now.*)

Narrator   Though they bore his name, the late Vincent Meehan was not the twins' father /

Nell Nell   *they knew this.*

Narrator   Nell Nell wouldn't tolerate secrets of any stripe.

Nell Nell   *Everyone had the right to be born into their own story.*

Narrator   The widow Meehan didn't hold back /

(**Tiernan** *storms into the front room, hands over his ears.* **Nell Nell** *opens a manuscript.*)

Nell Nell   *Told the boys they were the product of a long, loveless affair that neither party could understand or escape.*

Narrator   At least she could blame the years of her drinking.

Nell Nell   *Her pregnancy put an end to both. The day her boys were born her story had a true beginning.*

Narrator   She boxed off her past, juggled her babbies by day, typed up manuscripts while they slept /

Nell Nell   (*marks manuscript with a pen*)   *Making improvements as she went, like an editor . . . only cheaper /*

Narrator   Nimble Fingers Typing Services was usually in the red.

Nell Nell   *Their father had always paid towards the twins /*

Narrator   even tried to have a relationship with them /

(**Ferdia** *enters the front room,* **Tiernan** *comes out of the bedroom.*)

Ferdia   *boring afternoons in weird places where no one would see them.*

Nell Nell   *At seven, Ferdia refused to see his father again. Tiernan followed suit.* (*Shrugs.*) *It was their choice. So it had always been just the three of them /*

Ferdia   *and a house full of deadbeats and space cadets.*

(**Maeve**, **Marcus**, **Flix** *and* **Spangles** *come out of their rooms, mill about the place.*)

Narrator   The detritus of Nell Nell's ongoing identity quest formed the tenantry of misfits and non-belongers.

Marcus (*at* **Spangles**)   Paranoid pseudo-anarchists /

Spangles (*at* **Marcus**)   middle-class Maoists /

Maeve (*proudly*)   hairy feminists /

Flix (*winking*)   working-class heroes

Nell Nell   *Always the motherless who stayed behind.*

Narrator   No. 1 was the last house standing on the Parade. Sandwiched 'twixt the flat complexities of Arthur Gately Gardens and Pearse D'Alton Mansions. Propped up by steel girders /

Maeve   held together by bad carpentry and butter vouchers /

Nell Nell   and ghosts.

Ghost Bridie (*bored*)   **Only herself for the most part . . . and Ned Cummins' footsteps, no talking to them.**

Spangles   But thanks to the pin in the electric meter /

Nell Nell   they were the first ever residents to be warm /

Spangles   as long as they dodged the meter man /

Marcus   who called every eight weeks /

Maeve   and Spangles' paranoia went off the charts.

(**Spangles** *opens the door, checks the street, then ushers* **Flix** *out hurriedly.* **Nell Nell** *turns to her boys.*)

Nell Nell (*stunned*)   Not leaving leaving . . . What about university?

Narrator   Tiernan got himself expelled for selling magic mushrooms but Ferdia had won a scholarship.

Ferdia   It's just for the summer, probably . . . I can defer.

Nell Nell   Where'd you get the money?

Ferdia (*shrugs*)   I just kind of asked Dad for it.

Narrator   Nell Nell had long dreaded the day when her boys would leave each other.

Nell Nell   *Tiernan needed Ferdia in ways none of them could understand.*

Narrator   But now Ferdia had finally given in to his restless urgency to find the world /

Ferdia   *to which he truly belonged*

(*Phone rings in the hallway.* **Maeve** *thunders down the stairs.*)

Nell Nell   You go fly, Ferdia, I'll look out for Tiernan. (*They hug.*)

Maeve (*on phone*)   Hello, Women's Information Line, Maeve speaking . . . Go burn in hell yourself, you old bigot!

She slams the phone down.

Scene Two: 'The Val Mooney Television Show'

(*TV studio.* **Fr. Iggy** *sings, urging the audience to join in.*)

Fr. Iggy (*singing*)

   Where's your momma gone (Where's
   your momma gone)
   Little baby bird, (Little baby bird)

(*The* **Ghost Misfortunate** *enters and stands beside* **Iggy***; he redoubles his efforts, but she rattles him.*)

Fr. Iggy (*singing*)

   Where's your momma gone (Where's
   your momma gone)
   Far far away far far awayayay
   Far far away far far awayayay

(**Iggy** *starts coughing, the lights come up on TV host,* **Val Mooney**, *sitting beside* **Dinny Flood**.)

Val Mooney   Our very own sing-a-long priest, Fr. Iggy Rigney, ladies and gentlemen.

(*The audience clap.* **Iggy** *waves as he crosses over to sit beside* **Val** *and* **Dinny**. **Ghost Misfortunate** *shadows him.*)

Narrator   Val's stiff stage presence had translated brilliantly to television. *The Val Mooney Show* was the nation's most popular programme

Val Mooney   And now, finally, some good news from the North City Innards, Francis Cummins Bridge was opened today by my guests Fr. Iggy Rigney and Dinny Flood, T.D.

Dinny Flood   It would never have been built without Fr. Iggy's dogged persistence, Val.

Val Mooney   And Father Ig, we know from your bestselling memoir *The Boy from Tubbercurry Street* that you were born and reared in the North City Innards.

Fr.Iggy   You could leave your door open back then. Nowadays . . . joyriding, lawlessness, the youth have lost their way –

Flix (*from the audience*)   Val, Flix Kelly from Community Action North Innards . . . our young people see no future, they can't get jobs because they come from Arthur Gately Gardens or Pearse D'Alton Mansions. We need investment /

Dinny Flood   The well is dry!

Flix   And what about your plans for a motorway that will wipe out the community you represent?

Dinny   Rubbish! That's an out and out lie, Val.

(*The TV show disappears.* **Flix** *makes his way to O'Rehilly.*)

Narrator   Inserting himself into *The Val Mooney Show* was a coup for Flix Kelly.

Flix   *Though they'd shut him up before he could say what they never would. That our kids were not their kids.*

Narrator   And in over a hundred years precious little had changed in the streets about O'Rehilly Parade.

Scene Three: 'Untwinned'

(*O'Rehilly Parade.* **Nell Nell**, **Maeve**, **Spangles**, **Marcus**, **Flix** *are at the door.* **Tiernan** *hangs back.*)

Narrator   'Twas a dog of a day when Ferdia Meehan joined the wave of migrants headed for a New York they'd seen on TV, armed with only holiday visas and a cultural inability to answer a direct question.

Tiernan   *He couldn't look Ferdia in the eye as he left.*

Nell Nell   (*shouting*)   Don't forget to ring . . . reverse the charges.

Spangles   You won't know yourself without him, eh, T?

Narrator   The endless summer stretched out ahead of Tiernan /

Tiernan   *his dumbfuck pro-employment course, weekends collecting glasses in the Carter's. Him, on his own, living with this shower of wingnuts.*

Nell Nell   Wait and see, the summer'll fly by. He'll be back before you know it.

Tiernan   Ferdia's never coming back.

(*A crack of thunder. Rain.*)

Narrator   The summer of '81 had begun.

(*The phone rings.* **Tiernan** *goes to answer it as* **Maeve** *runs down the stairs.*)

Maeve   It's for me.

Tiernan   How do you know 'til you answer it?

Maeve   'Cos Spangles wrote the phone-line hours on the wall!

(**Maeve** *points to timetable on wall.* **Tiernan** *turns to* **Spangles**.)

Tiernan   Very into rules for an anarchist.

Maeve   Shhhh . . . (*On phone.*)   Hello, Women's Information Line, Maeve speaking . . . That's ok . . . take your time.

(**Ned**-*like,* **Tiernan** *loiters by the stairwell watching* **Maeve**. **Ghost Bridie** *goes into the privy with her chamber pot.*)

Tiernan   *Even if Maeve wasn't a hypocrite like the rest of them, she was still a wind-up, with her armpits and her arguments and the bang of patchouli off her.*

Narrator   Still, he hung on each word of her broad Cork accent . . .

Maeve (*on phone*)   The clinic in Liverpool is the closest.

Tiernan   *She was a dog compared to the birds in the blue movies they showed after-hours in the Carter's.*

(**Tiernan** *grabs his bondage jacket and heads for the door.* **Spangles***, who's been observing, pulls him aside.*)

Spangles   Sometimes I swear blind I can hear someone pissing into a bucket in my bedroom, I turn on the light and there's nothing there.

Tiernan   So?

Spangles   If you let stuff go round and round in your head it feels real, but it's not, man, trust me.

(**Tiernan** *shakes his head, marches out; 'Made in Liarland' is painted on the back of his jacket.* **Spangles** *sighs, goes to his room. In the front room* **Nell Nell** *looks out the window at* **Tiernan**, *who lights a fag.*)

Narrator   Since Ferdia left, Nell Nell saw shades of her old destructive streak in Tiernan /

Nell Nell   *Knew what you didn't know could hurt you more than what you did.*

Narrator   'Twasn't only a house could be haunted. She worried /

Nell Nell   *that it was in his genes.*

Narrator   In the roundabouts of his language, lurking in his silences . . . waiting only for to strike.

Scene Four: 'Times Squared'

(*Times Square. City sounds, rain.* **Ferdia** *stands in spotlight, multi-coloured dots swirl around. This scene echoes Arthur's breakdown (Act One, Scene Twenty-One) Now, the context is joyous but the echoes portentous.*)

Narrator   The statue of Fearless Father Duffy stood majestically in the mouth of Broadway and Seventh. Times Square in the midnight rain was a wonder to Ferdia.

Ferdia   *Flashing neon raindrops refracted off the windows, multi-coloured puddles shimmered with possibility /*

Narrator   Ragged hustlers and grifters fell in behind swanks from the Upper West Side.

Ferdia   Young ones smoking huge cigars. Hookers cat-called a guy sashaying past in a cocktail dress.

(*A shriek.* **Ferdia** *looks upward.*)

Ferdia   A topless woman teetered on a high-up window ledge, screaming into the night.

Narrator   Shrieking. Laughter. Howling. All tumbled atop one another /

Ferdia   policemen ran backwards.

Narrator   As he turned to look, Ferdia caught sight of a young man /

Ferdia   alone, in the glass doorway /

Narrator   The second split
in two.

Narrator/Ferdia   He saw own his reflection /

Ferdia   smiling radiantly back at him.

Narrator   Ferdia Meehan's insides erupted in a stormburst
of ecstasy.

Ferdia   Ireland couldn't drag him backwards from here.
His brilliant life was beginning at last.

Narrator   And all thoughts of Tiernan were swept away
like dust on th'upswell of a hot Manhattan wind. As if to
mark his unshackling /

Ferdia   gunfire ripped across the street A skinny
black lad dropped like a toy soldier.

Narrator   Behind him the topless woman jumped from the
ledge landing in a soundless heap on the sidewalk.

Scene Five: 'Tiernan the Roadie'

(*Playing area,* **Tiernan** *walks on with his guitar.* **Debbie** *follows.*)

Narrator   When Tiernan found out the Battle of
the Bands was being judged by his idols The Angelus /

Tiernan   *he bottled out of playing solo. A shower of Southriver
poxbottles in leather and lipstick won.*

Debbie   Hey, you, with the guitar!

Tiernan   *He'd seen her inside hanging off Bong, the singer from
The Angelus.*

Debbie   How come you didn't you play tonight?

Tiernan   My band broke up.

Debbie   Were you The Bastard Meehans? (*He nods.*) Cool name. Are you from around here?

Tiernan   *She certainly wasn't* // Yeah, near enough, O'Rehilly Parade.

Debbie   My Grandad opened his first shop in Poke's Alley.

Tiernan   That's all knocked down now // *Why was she talking to him?*

Debbie   You wouldn't do us a favour and walk me as far Pearse D'Alton Mansions?

(**Tiernan** *nods and they walk off together.* **Debbie** *exits,* **Tiernan** *waits.*)

Narrator   Tiernan walked Debbie to the flat complexities a few times /

Tiernan   *before she asked him to go for her . . .*

Debbie (*entering*)   You know The Angelus need a roadie, I can put a word in for you with Bong.

Tiernan   *She was kind of going out with Bong.*

Debbie   But like not in an official way. We're not good for one another but we can't keep apart either /

Tiernan   *unless Bong's official girlfriend was around.*

Narrator   Then Debbie would be all over Tiernan.

Debbie (*puts her arms around him*)   I gave your demo tape to Bong, do I not get a hug for that?

Tiernan (*hugs her awkwardly*)   *He didn't mind being used, he'd nothing else going on, but he wasn't thick.*

Narrator   He was a small, spotty, speccy-four-eyed, scum-punk and neither Debbie or /

Tiernan   *even the grottiest mots who followed The Angelus would be caught rapid with him.*

Band Guy (*from off*)   Hey . . . you with the bondage kaks. Bong's looking for you.

Narrator   Like all outcasts, Tiernan was only short of an invitation.

Tiernan (*surprised*)   *He became The Angelus' kind-of roadie.*

Narrator   More trips to the flats followed.

(**Jamesy Lawless** *enters; they do a quick deal.* **Tiernan** *is upbeat throughout, glad to have meaning and purpose.*)

Tiernan   *He got it off Jamesy Lawless* /

Jamesy Lawless   who got it off Dotsy /

Tiernan (*surprised*)   *who got it off Scobie O'Neill?*

Narrator   Bong said nothing about his demo tape, not that they talked. Ever.

(*A* **Band Guy** *comes on;* **Tiernan** *hands him the stuff, but it's clear he isn't invited to the inner sanctum.*)

Band Guy   Good man, there's a snakebite waiting for you at the bar from Bong.

Angelus Fan (*from off*)   Tiernan, man, over here!

Tiernan   *People who'd never noticed him before were glad to see him coming. And not because Ferdia was walking in front of him.*

Narrator   The summer was turning out ok after all.

Tiernan   *He jacked in his pro-employment course, stopped writing angry songs for no one to sing.*

(*He unhooks the chains of his bondage kaks.*)

Narrator   Tiernan Meehan hung up his chains. He made peace with one of life's great truths

Tiernan (*shrugs happily*)   *People were selfish fucks.*

Scene Six: 'The House of Hibernia'

(*January 1982. O'Rehilly Parade. Front room.* **Maeve**, **Marcus**, **Flix** *are all reading.* **Spangles** *rolls a joint.* **Ghost Bridie** *sits by the window, bored.* **Nell Nell** *enters reading a letter.*)

Narrator   'Twas January 1982 agin' the house that had built the nation was set to be eaten by its own creation.

(*Shocked,* **Nell Nell** *hands the letter to* **Flix**.)

Flix   I knew it! Dinny Flood's motorway is going to run straight through O'Rehilly Parade.

Ghost Bridie (*gasps*)   **Agin' the house was gone, her wish would be used up . . .**

Narrator   And Nell Nell having no people to belong to, belonged to this place.

Nell Nell   Technically the house isn't mine. It was left to my mother, Hibernia, and there's no record of her death, so she can't agree to it . . .

Marcus   A compulsory purchase order overrides everything.

Flix   We'll appeal it, get the Doylesevers and Arthur Gately Pipe Band on board. Dragging it through the court will take years, anything could have happened by then.

(**Flix** *takes the letter and leaves.*)

Maeve   So you never found out what happened to your mother, Nell Nell?

Marcus   There must be some record of the daughter of Arthur Gately.

Maeve   Read the history books, Marcus, women don't exist.

Nell Nell   This photo of us is the only proof I have of her existence. My father told me she'd died in childbirth.

Maeve   Eh . . . she clearly didn't.

Nell Nell (*sighs*)   Probably wanted to save me the pain of knowing she'd abandoned me.

Spangles   I was seven when my Mum put me in the children's home, last I ever saw of her.

(**Nell Nell** *reaches for his hand*. **Maeve** *stands on the creaky floorboard*.)

Maeve   My thesis is about the hidden history of women. I could try looking for Hibernia?

Nell Nell (*firmly*)   If she wanted to find me, I'm still exactly where she left me.

Ghost Bridie   Dead or alive, she'd not find her if the house itself was gone.

(*This registers with* **Nell Nell**.)

Maeve   I look for what isn't there. There's always a fragment, a footprint, an echo of something.

(*The echo of* **Ned Cummins**' *footsteps*. **Nell Nell** *turns suddenly in that direction*.)

Narrator   Still, th'untold story ached for resolution.

Nell Nell   Ok, Maeve. Maybe you'll have better luck than me.

Ghost Bridie   He knew how to use his footsteps to best effect, you had to give Ned Cummins that.

Scene Seven: 'Twelve Bells'

(*Street Bells of The Angelus sound, guitars grind between each bell*. **Debbie** *is comforted by* **Southriver Heads**.)

Narrator   Nothing prepared Tiernan for the sight of Debbie standing on the pavement /

Tiernan   *roaring and crying,*
surrounded by Southriver Heads /

Son of Judge   the sons of judges /

Music Journalist   music
journalists /

Girlfriend of Asshole in Band   girlfriends of assholes
in bands.

Narrator   It was worse than bad news . . .

Debbie (*distraught*)   The Angelus got a record deal and
moved to London /

Son of a Judge   no farewell gig /

Music Journalist   no forwarding address.

Narrator   The pus in Tiernan's pimples boiled with
self-recrimination.

Tiernan   *He knew they'd been using him and he'd gone along*
with it anyway.

Narrator   A sniff of good fortune coming to native sons
had a unifying effect on the Southriver Heads

Music Journalist   The Angelus could grind their guitars
but they'd nothing to say /

Son of a Judge   only draw a crowd in a kip like
Dublin /

Girlfriend of Asshole in Band   'Twelve Bells' was their
one decent tune.

Music Journalist   They'd be home by Christmas.

Narrator   Tiernan knew The Angelus were never
coming back.

Tiernan   *And he was nothing again. Worse, nothing squared.*

(**Future Ghost A&R man** *enters, hair in a man-bun, suit, British*
accent, FaceTiming into an iPhone.)

Future Ghost A&R Man   I'm in Dublin for the Nothing Squared gig? Yeah, he's still refusing to sign to a major label . . . it's worth a try . . .

Tiernan   What's this looper speaking into?

(*The* **Southriver Heads** *all look at* **Tiernan**. *He immediately becomes self-conscious; they don't see what he sees.*)

Son of a Judge   I think your mate is tripping, Debbie /

Narrator   The Southriver Heads split, leaving Tiernan standing on the pavement with yer man nobody else could see.

Future Ghost A&R Man   Amazing songwriter . . . unbelievable backstory.

(**Future Ghost A&R Man** *turns around, accidently elbowing* **Tiernan** *in the face. Tiernan doubles over holding his nose.* **Future Ghost A&R Man** *walks off. When Tiernan looks up there's nothing there.*)

Narrator   By the time Tiernan looked up, whateveritwas had vanished.

Tiernan   *How could he be tripping when he hadn't taken anything?*

Narrator   Only ever taken magic mushrooms the once, when Ferdia forced him into it /

Tiernan (*relieved*)   *That was it . . . he must be having a flashback.*

Narrator   But his nose throbbed and now it was starting to bleed.

(**Tiernan** *puts his hand to his nose, sees the blood. He storms off.*)

Scene Eight: 'Double-Faced Dinny'

(*Outside O'Rehilly Parade.* **Flix** *enters making his way to O'Rehilly.* **Dinny** *enters, furious.*)

Narrator   By the time summer rolled around there'd been another election.

Flix   Dinny Flood lost his seat by forty-seven votes!

Dinny   *That community bollix* **Flix Kelly** *had run as an independent and split the vote. Neither of them got in.*

Flix   Mission accomplished. O'Rehilly Parade lives to fight another day.

(**Flix** *enters house.* **Ghost Bridie** *on the step, smoking her pipe, watches a* **Speculator** *enters, looking at the house.*)

Dinny   *The honcho said it wasn't winning that defined you but what you did when you lost. The drudge work of nation-building he called it . . . palm-greasing, rule curling, words of warning.*

Speculator   How come this house hasn't been knocked?

Dinny   That place is history. The new road will run straight through it and down to the docks. We still control the city council, so your bid is safe.

(**Speculator** *nods and firmly shakes* **Dinny**'s *hand, leaves. Sound of a police siren in the distance.*)

Dinny   *This dump had always been a cesspit of crime. And still people wanted to stay here? Perpetuating their misery, singing songs celebrating their generational alcoholism. If they couldn't learn from the past then that was just natural selection. This was more than development, it was evolution. (Exits.)*

(**Future Ghost on Segway**, *talking into his watch, zips across the stage.* **Ghost Bridie** *cannot believe her eyes.*)

Future Ghost On Segway   I'll see you at the rooftop bar in The Tubbercurry, cocktails are awesome there.

Ghost Bridie   Babe of Bethlehem! She'd never seen the like, dead nor alive . . .

Narrator   Whateveritwas didn't see Bridie Meehan either. For once, her fear out measured her curiosity /

Ghost Bridie (*going back in*)   **She hightailed it back inside to the safety of her rightful.**

Scene Nine: 'Identity Theft'

(*The Carter's Arms. 'Twelve Bells' plays in the background.*)

Narrator   'Twelve Bells' entered the British charts at number 5. The Angelus were everywhere

Tiernan   *And he was back where he started, collecting glasses in The Carter's poxy Arms /*

(*The* **Drinkers** *form the Carter's Arms.*)

Narrator   where all talk was of the mayhem unfolding in the flats.

Drinker One   Strangers queuing outside Scobie O'Neill's flat day and night.

Drinker Three   Like the walking dead

Drinker Two   Collapsing all over the stairwells.

Drinker Three   A load of the mothers got together.

Drinker Two   Flix Kelly persuaded the men to join in.

Drinker Three   Families Against they're calling themselves.

Drinker One   Checking who's coming in and out of the Complexities

(*In the playing area a* **Man** *and* **Two Women** *push on an oil barrel; Families Against is written on it, flames inside. A* **Young Guy** *is stopped by the patrol,* **Jamsey Lawless** *swaggers past. The* **Drinkers** *try to get* **Tiernan***'s attention.*)

Drinker 2   They called Scobie to a meeting.

Drinker One   He didn't show up.

Drinker Three   Living like a king he is.

Drinker Two   And his neighbours getting robbed all around him.

Drinker Three   Neck on him like a jockey's bollix.

Drinker One   Families Against are going to march on his flat

Drinker Three   And he'll have to get out or be put out.

Drinker Two (*re* **Tiernan**)   Here . . . whatshisface?

Drinker Three (*shrugs*)   Hey, hair-oil, same again.

Narrator/Tiernan   *He felt the second split in two /*

Tiernan   *he saw himself as others did. Invisible.*

Narrator   Lickety spit, he done the mathematicals.

Tiernan (*sounding like* **Frankie**)   *If you weren't wanted you had to make yourself needed.*

Narrator   But what felt like a revelation to Tiernan was just an old clock ticking in a new body.

Scene Ten: 'Blackmail'

(*Mooney's sitting room.* **Irene Mooney** *walks on and gives* **Val** *a bunch of letters as she reads a postcard.*)

Irene   Val, there's a postcard from the girls!

Narrator   The Mooneys' teenage daughters were at GaelCamp for the first time.

Val Mooney   *The girls, when they finally got them, had transformed their lives.*

Narrator   In exchange, Fr. Iggy got to appear on *The Val Mooney Show* whenever he wanted.

Irene   They're singing 'Twelve Bells' in Irish for the final concert!

Narrator   Val's marriage to Irene had become a place of deep contentment and shared vision.

Val Mooney   *Family was everything to them.*

(**Val** *opens one of the letters; his face falls as he reads,* **Irene** *kisses his cheek and leaves.*)

Narrator   The letter threatened to blow up his whole life /

Val Mooney   *But he knew, against all his better judgement, he would send the money to the PO BOX.*

Narrator   There were some silences that had to be bought.

Scene Eleven: 'The Curse of the Irish'

(*Split scene: NYC/O'Rehilly Parade. In a spotlight* **Ferdia** *strikes a pose. We hear crowds, cameras flash, opera music.*)

Narrator   Ferdia Meehan had been in New York for thirteen months.

Ferdia   *Living in his worldly lover's West Village brownstone. Parties every night. Horny mornings. Lazy afternoons reading aloud to each other /*

Bricklayer (*V.O.*)   Yo, Irish, wake up!

(*Spotlight and ambient sounds disappear. A shovel is thrown on.* **Ferdia** *catches it and shovels, resentfully.*)

Narrator   He worked in construction . . . shovelling cement into the mixer. The lead singer in his own life /

Ferdia   *was the same as everyone else – Irish, illegal and struggling to make rent.*

Narrator   He lived with five builders from Mayo in Queens.

(*The shotgun house.* **The Mayos** *enter, buckled, crashing where they land.* **Ferdia** *feeds coins into the phone.*)

Mayo Mick   Fighting Irish, working ten-hour days /

Mayo Tom   sweating like bastards in the heat /

Mayo Pat   skulling drink by the bucketload /

Mayo Joe   in The Happy Shamrock or The Pot O'Gold.

Ferdia   Singing 'Twelve Bells' non-fucken-stop. Snoring and farting and shouting in their sleep.

Narrator   When summer hit, the stench in the tiny shotgun house was unbearable.

(*O'Rehilly Parade. Phone rings.* **Tiernan** *flips his finger at the ringing phone as he walks past and out the door.*)

Ferdia   *Tiernan pretended to be out whatever time he rang. He was an O-fucken-lympic sulker.*

Narrator   Truth was, without Tiernan's worship, Ferdia's confidence was ebbing away.

(*The Leather Feather. Spotlight comes up on* **Ferdia**. *The Mayo lads turn into* **Patrons** *of The Leather Feather.*)

Ferdia   Each visit to The Leather Feather brought fresh torment. He was made abundantly aware of /

Patron Two   his poor personal hygiene /

Patron One   his European teeth /

Patron Three   pale, freckled skin /

Patron Two   cute . . . from the eyes up.

Ferdia   *He was in the epicentre of the gay universe and he couldn't get a foothold.*

Narrator   Ferdia Meehan's desires did not make him desirable. He felt cursed by his Irishness.

Ferdia   *He became the worst of all things, desperate. Lunging at guys before they clocked his substandard teeth.*

Narrator   Before long, the darkroom beckoned.

(*Lights out, lighters click, grunts, moans heavy breathing.*)

Narrator   Wasn't exactly how he'd dreamed of losing the burden of his virginity but, as it turned out /

(*Lights come up.* **Ferdia** *stands alone.*)

Ferdia   He couldn't even get a ride in a darkroom. He wasn't just Irish, he was fucking Ireland.

Scene Twelve: 'Power to the People'

(*Split scene: O'Rehilly/street.* **Spangles**, **Maeve**, **Nell Nell** *are in the front room.* **Spangles** *smokes a joint. Outside,* **Flix** *and* **Marcus** *smoke; they have placards: one says 'Against', the other 'Families'.*)

Narrator   Maeve's search for Hibernia was infuriating.

Spangles   You need to relax.

(**Spangles** *offers* **Maeve** *the joint; she waves it away. He hands it toward* **Nell Nell** *but* **Ghost Bridie** *intercepts it.*)

(**Spangles** *and* **Nell Nell** *are too focused on* **Maeve** *to notice.*)

Maeve   This is all I've got . . . a few women named Gately I found in the court reports.

(*She opens her folder and motions* **Nell Nell** *and* **Spangles** *to read.* **Ghost Bridie** *tokes away: not her first joint.*)

Spangles   Bertha Gately, six months hard labour for attempting to scald her husband.

Nell Nell   Florrie Gately, a prostitute, hung for murder 1887 . . .

Maeve   That'd be going too far back. Women are a nightmare to keep track of, they lose their names on marriage . . . always disappearing.

Spangles   Ciss Gately, a widow, got five months for the theft of two large hams /

Nell Nell   Honor Gately, an abortionist, penal servitude for life /

Ghost Bridie   and a seat at Lucifer's table. The vixen.

(**Nell Nell** *seems to hear* **Ghost Bridie** *who passes the joint back to* **Spangles***: too engrossed/stoned to register.*)

Maeve   Nothing we can link to Hibernia. I need more than loose threads. And so many births went unregistered back then /

Ghost Bridie   it cost money and so many of the little scraps never saw their first birthday. (*Sighs heavily.*) **To be born was to die and no knowing the measure 'twixt the two.**

(**Maeve** *relents and takes the joint off* **Spangles**, *a deep drag, lets out a loud sigh of frustration with the smoke.*)

Narrator   Maeve was going to have to get an extension on her thesis.

(*Outside Rehilly.* **Tiernan** *enters, a new arrogance about him, shades of* **Frankie** *in his voice.*)

Narrator   Outside O'Rehilly, Families Against were cleansing the flats of sellers. It was Tiernan /

Tiernan   *who told them Jamesy Lawless had taken over when Scobie O'Neill got put out.*

Flix   We're marching on Lawless after the meeting.

Tiernan   He got two warnings already.

Debbie (*from off*)   Hi, Tiernan.

(*They all look around.* **Debbie** *steps out of the shadows,* **Tiernan** *is blindsided.*)

Tiernan   Ah, Debbie, hiya. Yous go on, I'll catch up.

(**Flix** *and* **Marcus** *leave. In the playing area the* **Southriver Heads** *appear; they look around expectantly.*)

Narrator   Though the Southriver Heads had finished with Tiernan, he hadn't finished with them /

(*Leaving* **Debbie** *outside the house,* **Tiernan** *goes over to the* **Southriver Heads**; *they're pleased to see him coming.*)

Tiernan   *They didn't give two colours of shite about The Angelus, just shared a goo for it* /

Narrator   for Opiumistan's chief export . . . the Painmelter

(*Handshaking, backslapping and discreet dealing goes on, money changes hands.*)

Tiernan   *They didn't mind being charged over and above. They were discreet, too* /

Son of Judge   given they'd plenty to lose.

Tiernan   *Soon as he'd offloaded he'd slip back across the river.*

Tiernan/Narrator   Knew every back-alley and cut-through in the city /

(**Tiernan** *is unsettled by the* **Narrator**'*s mindreading but doubles down.*)

Tiernan   *changed his route regular. He never carried anything back to O'Rehilly.*

Narrator   Covered his tracks Northriver in Families Against.

Tiernan   *He hadn't got this far for a Rathrockilly rich kid to ruin everything*

Debbie   I wouldn't have come, only I'm sick Tiernan I need /

Narrator   Rages older than Tiernan surged through him. The bad blood of both sides boiling as he /

Tiernan (*surprised by what he's doing*)   *reefed her aside, squared up to her /*

Debbie (*frightened*)   *she was shaking.*

Narrator   And in spite of hisself, Speccy Meehan liked the feel.

Tiernan   *Nobody'd ever been scarified of him before.*

Narrator   Wouldn't be the first about the Parade found harbour in the tormenting of a person defenceless.

Tiernan   Take yourself and your problems back to Rathrockilly, we've enough of our own round here.

(*Chant of 'Lawless Out' in the distance. He lets go of her.* **Debbie** *runs off.*)

Narrator   Tiernan scarce knew what, or who had come over him /

Tiernan   *But she was gone. He wasn't thick enough to think that'd be the end of her /*

Narrator   The Painmelter had her in its grip. She'd be back.

Tiernan   *Her Da's chemist shops were broken into every other night in the city innards. Time he found out what was going on in his own home. There couldn't be many Al Mostafas in the phone book. One day, she'd probably thank him for it.* (*Shouts as he exits.*) LAWLESS OUT! LAWLESS OUT!

Scene Thirteen: 'The Misfortune Teller'

(*Parish house.* **Fr. Iggy** *enters with his guitar. He yawns. A faint sound of a baby crying unsettles him a little.*)

Narrator   The late nights were taking their toll on the Sing-a-Long Priest.

Fr. Iggy   *He was gigging non-stop for the 'Save the Not-yet-born' campaign.*

Narrator   Even though the doctor told him he had months rather than years.

(**Fr. Iggy** *goes into his lounge.* **Ghost Misfortunate** *sits reading.*)

Ghost Misfortunate   Sorry I didn't make it to the show tonight. I couldn't put this down, (*reads the cover*) **'The Boy from Tubbercurry Street'.**

Fr. Iggy   *He understood their function, particularly for saint-weaving, but he'd never been one for apparitions.*

Ghost Misfortunate   The mix of fact and fiction jars a little. Maybe you should have hired a ghost writer?

Fr. Iggy   It's a bestseller, so you're on your own there.

Ghost Misfortunate   We're all waiting for you, with our empty arms and broken hearts.

Fr. Iggy (*snapping*)   Well yis should have thought of that before yis laid down like dogs in a field.

Housekeeper (*off*)   Father Iggy, are you alright there?

Fr. Iggy   Grand Mrs. C. Grand. Just practising a new routine.

(**Iggy** *deliberately keeps his back to the* **Ghost Misfortunate** *as he turns off the light.*)

Fr. Iggy   You don't scare me.

Ghost Misfortunate   Not yet. Dying is harder than you think.

(*In the playing area* **Val Mooney** *and* **Detective Troy** *meet and shake hands, they walk off together.*)

Scene Fourteen: 'Ferdia's Revolution'

(NYC. Shotgun house. Snoring, farting, shouting as the **Mayo Builders** *sleep.* **Ferdia** *stumbles in half asleep.)*

Narrator   Failing to acquire the life of his dreams, Ferdia's dreams themselves began to change.

Ferdia   *A fresh horror descended on him.*

Narrator   The romanticising of home. Salt and vinegar on that?

Ferdia   *Sausages-in-batter grew three times their size /*

Narrator   endless grey winters unremembered.

Ferdia   *He was losing his mind. There was nothing at home . . . except home.*

Narrator   Tiernan's cloying dependence. His adoration, too.

Ferdia   *The long-distance sulk was working. But if he gave in now . . . he'd never be free*

(A tattered book is pushed on stage. **Ferdia** *picks it up, and as he opens it,* **Ghost George Doyle** *enters.)*

Narrator   He bought a dog-eared copy of *Novelbuke* by George Doyle from a kerbside huckster.

Ferdia   To Honor in lieu of debt to you – George. *(Reads some.) It was deranged gibberish /*

Ghost George   **except for the sublime passages where the language somersaulted with such free-wheeling joy that /**

Ferdia   *it made him long to be in earshot of his city.*

Ghost George   George Doyle's Dublin sang to him from the top of the century, revealing the city /

Ferdia   *not as the backward, filthy dump it was /*

Ghost George   but intimate and expansive, wealthy with words, extravagant in expression /

Ferdia   *it was in language where Dublin's freedom lay.*

Ghost George   The rhythm of the words was the rhythm of the city was the rhythm of his soul.

Ferdia   *It wasn't Ireland he hankered for, it was Dublin. He'd always be wallpaper here. He lacked context. He could be mincing around college by October. Even re-form The Bastard Meehans for Tiernan.*

(**Mayo Tom** *rises from the pile of snorting, farting bodies. He is wearing an Angelus T-shirt.*)

Ferdia   *He spent his last night in New York dancing on the tables in The Happy Shamrock /*

Mayo Tom   belting out 'Brave Arthur Gately', you were. Some man for one man.

Ferdia   *He'd rather die than end up like this shower, strung-out on fake Irish tomfuckery.*

Mayo Tom   Why are you going back? You've only started having the craic.

Ferdia   Ah, you know . . . I'm a twin. My brother needs me.

Mayo Tom   You're free here to . . . do . . . your thing. Nobody looking at you, talking about you.

Ferdia   I want people to talk about me. I want people to look at me.

Mayo Tom   You know they'll never let you back in if you've overstayed?

Ferdia   Yep. New York isn't my city. My revolution is where I left it, in Dublin.

Mayo Tom   I'd say it's still waiting for you, in fairness like.

(**Ferdia** *smiles,* **Tom** *too. Then* **Tom** *shoves out his hand for a manly shake.*)

Mayo Tom   G'luck so. With yer revolution. (*He leaves.*)

Ferdia   *Dublin wasn't all he was cracking it up to be but at least he wasn't going back to poxy Mayo.*

Scene Fifteen: 'Mount-of-Joy'

(*Mount-of-Joy/street.* **Tiernan** *sits in holding cell. All his ancestral defences down; he is himself and terrified.*)

(*During the scene, the* **Southriver Heads** *wait around, expectantly, before giving up and drifting off.*)

Narrator   In Mount-of-Joy Jail Tiernan sat trembling in the holding cell. /

Tiernan   *His secrets had felt like power, as if he made the rules.*

Narrator   Rules aplenty where he was heading now. He wanted to scream /

Tiernan   *It wasn't me* /

Narrator   who blackmailed his father for the money to get himself started /

Tiernan   *It wasn't me*

Narrator   got Debbie Al Mostafa frogmarched off to a de-drugification centre /

Tiernan   *It wasn't me* /

Narrator   gave Jamsey Lawless's name to Families Against while he plied his trade Southriver /

Tiernan   *It wasn't me* /

Narrator   who didn't even spend the money /

Tiernan   just stashed it in his un-played guitar.

Narrator   Agin' the guardians arrested him for blackmail /

Tiernan   *they found all the wraps of Painmelter* /

Narrator   And the secret lives of Tiernan Meehan blew up in his face. His only defence?

Tiernan (*pathetically*)   *It wasn't me . . .*

Narrator   There'd been taller stories put before Dublin judges. But if it wasn't Tiernan Meehan getting his his own back on the world /

Tiernan (*ashamed*)   *on Val Mooney, on Ferdia* /

Narrator   then who was it?

Tiernan (*terrified*)   *The door opened* /

(*A* **Screw** *enters, motions to* **Tiernan** *to follow him. Gate opening, prison sounds.* **Two Prisoners** *mop the floors.*)

Tiernan   *and the screw led him to the landing in the main jail* /

Prisoner One   Prisoners stuffed, four, five and six to a cell /

Prisoner Two   all served by a single slop bucket.

Tiernan   *The putrid stench infected the air* /

Prisoner One   seeped into the walls /

Prisoner Two   crept under the doors.

Tiernan   *A rancid stew of shit, piss, boiled meat* /

Narrator   semen and violence. A far cry from the ramshackle comforts of O'Rehilly Parade and Nell Nell's overloving arms.

Screw (*opens cell door*)   There's four already in this cell, you'll be sleeping on the floor.

Tiernan   *The three other lads looked up to the sham on the top bunk. It was Jamesy-fucken-Lawless.*

(**Tiernan** *backs away but the* **Screw** *pushes him in and slams the door.*)

Scene Sixteen: 'Busted'

(*O'Rehilly Parade.* **Guardians** *burst into the house.* **Ghost Bridie** *retreats back upstairs with her chamber pot.*)

Narrator   The Guardians piled into the house, all beef and bog accents.

Detective Troy   Detective Martin Troy. I've a warrant to search the premises.

(*A* **Guardian** *goes upstairs. The* **Ban Guardian** *steps on the creaky floorboard en route to* **Tiernan**'s *room.*)

Detective Troy   Tiernan Meehan lives here.

Nell Nell   Yes, I'm his mother.

Detective Troy   He's in custody.

Nell Nell   What for?

Detective Troy   Blackmail, resisting arrest, possession and supply of Painmelter.

Marcus   That's ridiculous, this is a stitch up because he's in Families Against . . .

Ban Guardian   Is this his guitar?

Nell Nell   Yes.

Ban Guardian   This bag of cash was stuffed inside, Marty.

(**Ban Guardian** *steps on the creaky floorboard again, as she goes off searching for more evidence.*)

Detective Troy (*to the* **Guardian**)   Check under that floorboard, you.

(*A* **Guardian** *lifts the piece of floorboard; it easily gives way. Doesn't seem to be anything there.*)

Ban Guardian (*off*)   We've got a hash plant growing back here /

Spangles   That's for my own spiritual use, I'm a /

(*The phone rings.*)

Detective Troy   Shhhh. Hello? . . . Women's Information Line?

Maeve   That's me. (*Takes receiver.*)   I'm real sorry about this – would you be able to call back later? Thanks.

Detective Troy   An abortion hotline timetable on the wall. Well, isn't this place a hotbed of illegal activity.

Ban Guardian   This buck here has a dossier on Painmelter production in Opiumistan.

Marcus   It's for a political article about neo-colonial, post-imperialist mercenaries /

Detective Troy   Shhhh! Listen . . .

(*The sound of* **Ghost Bridie** *emptying her chamber pot into the toilet.* **Troy** *orders the* **Guardian**)

Detective Troy   Check the upstairs toilet. We're taking the lot of you down the station.

(*The* **Ban Guardian** *checks out under the floorboard; she finds something.*)

Ban Guardian   Got something here, boss.

(*The* **Ban Guardian** *produces* **Cornelius'** *stash tin.* **Nell Nell** *is shocked.* **Ban Guardian** *opens it.*)

Nell Nell   Daddy's tin.

Detective Troy   Bag it for prints. Ok everybody, stand against the wall.

(*Everyone lines up against the wall.* **Ferdia** *enters, bursts in the front door.*)

Ferdia   Surprise! I'm home!

Nell Nell   Ferdia!

Detective Troy   Search him.

(*A* **Guardian** *pins him against the wall.*)

Ferdia   Jesus . . . what's going on?

Ban Guardian   Nobody up here, boss.

(**Ghost Bridie** *flushes the toilet.*)

Detective Troy   Who's flushing the toilet, a ghost?
Check again.

(*A* **Man** *arrives, knocking at the open door.* **Detective Troy**
signals quiet, ready to pounce. The man steps in the door.)

Meter Man   Hello? ESB, I'm here to read the meter.
(*Blackout.*)

Scene Seventeen: 'Tosser's Pot'

(*Tosser's Pot.* **Ghost Granny** *and* **Ghost Florrie** *enter from
under the archway, still protecting their patch.*)

Narrator   If the city itself was a map of excuses, an
argument that didn't stack up, there was one model of
efficiency and purpose, impervious to the march of time . . .

Ghost Granny   Always the same down by Tosser's Pot

**Ghost Florrie   The punters were all sorts, the hewers just
the one.**

Ghost Granny   Those with nothing else to sell.

(*Dreamy music as* **Young One***, out of it, enters.*)

Young One   The Painmelter felt like a dream under warm
blankets. Time gliding.

Narrator   Mollified any pain as could be suffered /

Young One   you'd do
anything for it.

(**Dinny***, wearing a hat, collar pulled up, enters. He nods at the*
Young One *and they go under the archway.*)

Ghost Granny   Few'd risk a kneetrembler under th'archway these days.

Ghost Florrie   It was years since they'd put manners on the last punter.

(**Young One** *runs back on taking money from a wallet, flings it aside, runs away.* **Ghost Florrie** *picks it up.*)

Dinny (*off*)   Hey! Come back!

(**Ghost Florrie** *shows* **Ghost Granny** *the photos in the wallet.*)

Ghost Granny   His wife and child /

Ghost Florrie   some daughters more precious than others /

Ghost Granny   th'oul dirt-merchant.

(**Ghost Florrie** *throws the wallet down.* **Dinny** *enters in a fury, picks up the wallet, looks in it.* **Ghost Granny** *spits on her hands rubs them together then places her hand on his gut.* **Dinny** *winces at the sudden pain.*)

Dinny   Ow . . . Fuck! Jesus . . .

(*He takes a deep breath and exits.* **Ghost Granny** *and* **Ghost Florrie** *smile in satisfaction.*)

Scene Eighteen: 'Making Miracles'

(*Split scene: O'Rehilly Parade/Val's. In the house* **Marcus**, **Ferdia**, **Maeve**, **Spangles** *are shivering with cold.* **Ghost Bridie** *is wrapped in a blanket.*)

Narrator   The solicitor reckoned Tiernan was looking at three to four years. If he got bail it'd be a miracle. And miracles cost money . . .

(*Val's driveway.* **Nell Nell** *enters.*)

Nell Nell   *If it hadn't been for Tiernan's blackmail charge she'd never have thought of approaching him.* // Val

(**Val** *is stopped in his tracks as* **Nell Nell** *stands in his way.*)

Narrator   Valentine Mooney put up no resistance /

Val Mooney   *if he*
raised his voice, Irene or the girls would hear him.

Narrator   A current surged through Nell Nell as she /

Nell Nell   *did for*
her boy what she'd never been able to do for herself /

Narrator   play her
advantage.

Nell Nell   *Tiernan was his son too. Even if he had blackmailed him.*

Val Mooney   *Held hostage in his own driveway he agreed to her terms.*

Nell Nell   *She saw herself through his eyes then.*

Narrator   And Nell Nell finally understood what had drawn Val Mooney to her /

Nell Nell   *he hated her and always had.*

(**Val** *walks away.* **Nell Nell** *smirks in irony.*)

Nell Nell   *Another old story had a new beginning.*

Narrator   Val lingered a moment on the step /

Nell Nell   *before he*
opened the door into the life he'd made for himself

Val   in spite of her.

Scene Nineteen: 'Ex-o-bus (Movement of Jah Twins)'

(*Streets.* **Ferdia** *and* **Nell Nell** *greet* **Tiernan** *outside Mount-of-Joy. His glasses are missing; he's been roughed up.*)

Narrator   Val Mooney's connections to the higher-ups ensured his son got bail.

Ferdia   *Nothing prepared him for the sight of Tiernan . . .*

Tiernan (*shaken*)   *The fifteen months since they'd seen each other felt like fifty years.*

(**Nell Nell** *puts new specs on* **Tiernan**, *trying to hide her upset as she hugs him, then goes back to the house.*)

Tiernan   *They took the sixteen-hour journey on the Ex-o-bus to London.*

Ferdia   *Drank themselves sober with a gang of culchies coming back from a funeral.*

Narrator   Agin' they paid for the hostel in Crickleburn, scarce had a king's shilling.

Tiernan   *Stood in a pub doorway to shelter from the rain.*

Ferdia (*starts singing*)

   Brave Arthur Gately didn't die for this . . .

Narrator   Ferdia was waiting on his brother's word /

Tiernan (*smiles*)   *It uplifted him.*

Ferdia/Tiernan

   Politicians praying and priests on
   the piss

(*Now they go nuts, jumping around and playing air guitar and singing at the top of their voices.*)

Ferdia/Tiernan

   No rubber johnnies, no abortions
   Not enough chips in Gino's portions!

Tiernan/Ferdia

Ireland, Liarland, Ireland, Liarland

Narrator   Had to run for their lives from an English psycho with a Glasgow smile.

(*They run away, laughing and breathless.*)

Narrator   Tiernan was back with his other half /

Tiernan   *floating,*
above time, free.

Narrator   Thought he would die of bliss. And then The Bastard Meehans' British tour was over.

Ferdia   *He could scarce look him in the eye as he left. His shy defender, his blame-taker.*

(**Ferdia** *hugs him quickly, then turns away to leave.*)

Ferdia   *Tiernan wouldn't be ok and there was nothing he could do about it. Something cracked across his heart.* (*He exits.*)

Narrator   Ferdia faded from view and, in a moment's pass, all the fragile parts inside of Tiernan imploded /

Tiernan   *landing in a*
jagged heap of sharp ends and lonely corners.

Narrator   And the belief that he was arbitrarily cursed took root in Tiernan Meehan's troubled soul.

Scene Twenty: 'The Stash Tin'

(*Split scene: O'Rehilly Parade/cut-through.* **Ghost Bridie** *watches* **Nell Nell** *and* **Maeve** *assemble bits of paper.*)

Narrator   The Guardians returned Cornelius' stash tin, inside . . . his lost legacy /

Ghost Bridie   **tuppence ha'penny, a picture of Hitler and some rat-eaten scraps of paper /**

Maeve   the fragments /

Maeve   The lead they'd been searching for.

Ghost Bridie   Like patchwork they stitched it together.

Narrator   Guessed at the missing words the vermin had gnawed away.

Nell Nell   '. . . they will come for her Monday. Best if child'. . . . not? 'not present'?

Maeve (*squints*)   'Extra tablets will make' . . . 'things' . . . 'smoother'

Nell Nell   'As you have no parental obligation to the child'

(*Dissonant note sounds.* **Nell Nell** *reacts to it.*)

Nell Nell   So he wasn't my real father. Even my name is a lie.

(**Maeve** *squeezes* **Nell Nell**'s *hand.* **Nell Nell** *is more angry than upset.*)

Narrator   The signature was mottled but Nell Nell recognised the surname.

Nell Nell (*icily*)   Slavin. Doc Slavin.

(**Dr Slavin Jr** *enters from the side.* **Nell Nell** *leaves the house.* **Maeve** *follows to the cut-through and waits.*)

Narrator   Dr Slavin Junior had inherited his father's practice and his attitude. Told Nell Nell /

Dr Slavin Junior   it would be unethical to allow access to my father's files /

Nell Nell   *confirming their existence.*

Maeve   When Nell Nell pleaded for Hibernia's records for medical reasons, he assured her /

Dr Slavin Junior   No file could be found despite a thorough search of the basement /

Nell Nell   *revealing their location.*

(**Dr Slavin Jr** *and* **Nell Nell** *exit. A window smashes. In an echo Act Two, Scene Three we hear the sound of the struggle in cut-through as* **Nell Nell** *enters with the file.* **Maeve** *and* **Nell Nell** *hurry back to the house, to search the file.*)

Narrator   Slavin's files were an archive of the catastrophes of poverty, th'everyday opera of invisible lives /

Maeve   Pages of proof /

Nell Nell (*sombre*)   a file marked 'committals' /

Maeve   where they found the letter, the evidence /

Nell Nell   *of how men had the power to make or break a woman for no reason but one of their own choosing.*

Maeve   dated September 1935. Signed by Doc Slavin and Cornelius Considine.
Committing Hibernia to St Jude's Mental Asylum . . . for talking to the dead.

Nell Nell   *The hole inside her swelled, that an empty space could hold such pain.*

(**Spangles** *quietly embraces* **Nell Nell**. *Sound of a struggle, a woman hyper-ventilating, echoes.*)

Maeve   St Jude's closed down a few years ago but we won't give up until we find her, Nell Nell.

Ghost Bridie   Sucky seen someone getting dragged into the wagon at the cut-through to Tubbercurry Street.

(*The sounds of struggle stop. A beat of silence.*)

Nell Nell   She didn't leave me . . .

(*A few dissonant notes sound together, underscored with an soothing, airy sound. A sonic interpretation of a baby's cry and a mother's soothing shhhh.*)

Narrator   Hibernia Gately had been taken from her.

Scene Twenty-One: 'A Pig's Mickey'

(*The street.* **Young One** *collapses.* **Dinny** *enters, agitated, waiting for someone who is late or not coming. He winces, touching his stomach where* **Ghost Granny** *laid her hand, pops a Rennie.*)

Narrator   One year rolled into another and the Painmelter problem in the North Innards was overspilling.

Dinny   *Bag snatchers on Carnell Street, cameras getting reefed off tourists' necks on Doyleseve /*

Narrator   riots in the Mount-of-Joy /

Dinny   *that Families Against shower marching through the city with their cardboard coffins every fucking week! He'd made a pig's mickey out of justice, those were the honcho's words.*

Narrator   But it was what you did when you were losing that counted.

Dinny (*nods*)   *Exaggeration of the gunlicker involvement in Families Against had already taken seed.*

Flix (*furious*)   *Accusations of kangaroo courts and mob rule all over the papers!*

(**Addict** *approaches* **Dinny** *who takes him by the arm.* **Flix** *sees the* **Young One**, *goes to her aid.*)

Dinny   You know what you're going to say to the reporter?

Addict   I'd to pay £300 to a bloke or else he'd give my name to Families Against, get me thrun out.

Dinny   Good man // *He'd have the beat of Flix Kelly and his people power yet.* (*They exit.*)

Narrator   Only they weren't fighting for victory /

Flix   they were fighting for survival.

(**Flix** *carries the* **Young One** *off.*)

Scene Twenty-Two: 'The Slow Death of Iggy Rigney'

(Split scene: parish house/O'Rehilly Parade. **Iggy**'s *alone in the parish house.* **Spangles** *and* **Nell Nell** *in O'Rehilly.)*

Narrator   Death was looming but the boy from Tubbercurry Street was a stubborn wrestler.

Fr. Iggy   *He'd seen the 'Save the Not-yet-born' campaign fought and won. (Lights a cig).*

(A baby cries, more insistent than before. He lights a cig, dials the phone.)

Fr. Iggy   Hello, could I speak to Canon Fottrill please? . . . He's moved? Again? . . .

(He takes a sudden turn, collapses back into the chair. The **Ghost Misfortunate** *enters, picks up his cigarette.)*

Ghost Misfortunate   She left him a while so he could feel the full weight of his helplessness.

(She takes his cigarette. **Fr. Iggy** *tries to speak, to get up: he can do neither.)*

Ghost Misfortunate   Can't talk? As long as you can hear me, that's the main thing. My family arranged it all, you took me to England to have the baby so it could be adopted there. *(She takes a drag.)* **We were at Crickleburn Station when you slipped into a bookie's shop and I bolted. That not ring a bell? Sure I was only one of many. They never knew back home I'd kept him. For seven years I managed, until I didn't. He was all I had, my beautiful boy. I left him in a children's home, took the train to Brighton and walked into the sea.**

(O'Rehilly. **Spangles** *and* **Nell Nell** *look out into the distance. Dissonant notes sound.)*

Spangles   *Every day she didn't come my heart sank like a brick.*

Ghost Misfortunate   A female body washed ashore three weeks later was never identified.

Nell Nell   *The records from St Jude's went missing after it closed.*

Spangles   *There are holes inside a person that can never be filled.*

(*The* **Ghost Misfortunate** *puts out the cigarette, gets up to leave.* **Fr. Iggy** *struggles to speak.*)

Ghost Misfortunate   Easy now. You'll get used to being a silence. You've a while to go yet. When your time comes we'll all be waiting for you. And there are worse stories than mine.

Scene Twenty-Three: 'Ferdia Falls'

(*O'Rehilly. Basement. Disco music blares. Lights up, a party is under way in the back, out of view. Partygoers in the front smoking and drinking beer,* **Pleather Jimmy** *hovers about* **Ferdia** *by the door.*)

Narrator   While the country went to hell in a handcart, in the basement of O'Rehilly Parade /

Ferdia   The bang of poppers would knock you sideways.

Narrator   For a city that ran on alcohol, Dub-bel-lin closed punishingly early

Pleather Jimmy   By half eleven everyone was all tanked-up with nowhere to go.

Narrator   Ferdia had started his own club.

Ferdia   'Francis-in-Chains'. Gay Wrongs were as important as Gay Rights

(**Ferdia** *signals to* **Pleather Jimmy** *to let the straights in. He reluctantly does so.*)

Pleather Jimmy   They had to let the straights in, too. But they weren't allowed into the chain room.

Ferdia   Haunted by Holy Francis Cumming . . . the puns were endless.

Narrator   Ferdia was no longer wallpaper.

Ferdia   *He was the darling of the dental Armageddon that was Dublin. First in his year in college, won the George Doyle Medal for his essay on* Novelbuke /

Narrator   The busier he kept himself the less he thought about Tiernan

Ferdia   *They hadn't heard from him in over six months.*

(**Mayo Tom** *knocks.* **Pleather Jimmy** *opens the door.* **Ferdia** *has his back to him and doesn't see him.*)

Mayo Tom   How much is it in?

Ferdia   Two squids, three if you're straight, ten if you're a cop.

Mayo Tom   Here's two so.

Ferdia (*turning around*)   *Nothing prepared him for the sight of* **Tom** *standing there, his Mayo eyes twinkling.*

Mayo Tom   Howarya doing?

Ferdia   *They hadn't been this close to each other in three years.*

Mayo Tom   I thought I'd join your revolution so I did.

Ferdia   *Then quick as one minute falling into the next, his massive Mayo hands drew him close and all the world turned soft and warm.*

Narrator   For the first time since Tiernan went on the run, Ferdia forgot his other half.

Ferdia   *He was floating. Above time. Free.* (**Tom** *kisses* **Ferdia**.)

Scene Twenty-Four: 'Liarland'

(*Split scene: O'Rehilly Parade/Crickleburn. In O'Rehilly,* **Tom** *and* **Ferdia** *still kissing. In London a bomb goes off.*)

Narrator   With bombweavers on the loose, it was not a good time to be Irish in London.

Passerby   Fuck off home, Paddy.

(**Tiernan** *enters, he drains a can with the same Cummins family flourish. In O'Rehilly,* **Ferdia** *introduces* **Tom** *to* **Nell Nell**.)

Narrator   Tiernan drank to forget the life he'd lost. One year fell into two.

Tiernan   There was nothing to write home about.

Narrator   He measured his failure against The Angelus' spectacular success

Tiernan   '*Twelve Bells' had gone to number 27 in the States.*

Narrator   Now that he had success, Bong wanted credibility.

Tiernan   *Gone through five producers but now the album was ready. They'd sold out Crickleburn Apollo.*

(*In O'Rehilly,* **Ferdia** *reads* Novelbuke *to* **Tom**, *asleep with boredom. Audience roar as the band come on stage.*)

Bong (*from off*)   This is a song I wrote about Ireland.

Narrator   When the first few chords struck, a warm, familiar feeling washed over Tiernan.

Tiernan   *The crowd went ballistic as Bong started to sing*

Bong (*from off*)

Brave Arthur Gately didn't die for this,
Politicians praying and priests on the piss.

Narrator   Tiernan Meehan's stolen song ripped across the night sky over Crickleburn high street /

Tiernan (*gobsmacked*)   *The crowd already singing along by the second chorus*

Bong

Ireland, Liarland. Ireland, Liarland

(*O'Rehilly.* **Ferdia** *hears 'Liarland', has exactly the same reaction as Tiernan. He exits swiftly leaving Tom alone.*)

Narrator   An instant classic. The Angelus weren't just Irish now, they were Ireland.

Tom   *When Ferdia heard 'Liarland' on the radio, he went looking for Tiernan, alone. Didn't find him of course.*

Ferdia (*re-enters, continuing an argument*)   See! I told you there was no point in you coming, Tom.

Tom   I thought you might need me.

Ferdia   Yeah, right. Keep tabs on me more like.

Tom   *He'd a monumental pain in his Mayo hole with Tiernan fucking Meehan.*

(**Nell Nell** *appears, knows there's no news.* **Ferdia** *sighs, irritated.*)

Ferdia   We can prove Bong used Tiernan as his drug runner so he could steal his songs . . . the demo tapes are hard evidence and I know a lawyer /

Tom (*under his breath*)   and a plumber and a chef /

Ferdia (*to* **Tom**)   Seriously? Now? (*To* **Nell Nell**.) He'd have to come home, hand himself in until the trial. But he could be out in a year.

Tom   And he'd be loaded! 'Liarland' is never off the radio like.

Narrator   It felt like something to fight for. Until the news broke /

Tom   *Bong had died of an overdose in a Paris hotel.*

Ferdia   *He'd needed Tom then.* (**Tom** *embraces* **Ferdia**.)

Scene Twenty-Five: 'Down All the Days'

(*O'Rehilly Parade. Front room. Night.* **Ghost Bridie** *is fast asleep on the sofa. The pipes of the house gurgle.*)

(**Nell Nell** *opens the window.* **Ferdia** *watches her from the shadows.*)

Narrator   A year, two, fell a-top each other. The Francis Cummins Bridge collapsed, structural issues. Three days later, the sing-a-long priest finally popped his clogs. There'd been /

Nell Nell   *No word from Tiernan in over a year. He didn't know she'd changed her name to Gately, Ferdia too . . .*

Narrator   When the dreaded night-sweats descended, she'd stand by the window /

Nell Nell   *in a swirl of loneliness and ghosts*

(*The dissonant notes underscored with soothing breathy sounds play faintly underneath the following.*)

Narrator   Like all the Gatelys before her searching for a happier ending in a story bigger than any of them.

Of a curse, or a house or a city in time /

Nell Nell   *of a mother and child lost to each other . . .*

Narrator   And ongoing iterations thereof.

(*Sound fades.* **Ferdia** *enters and wraps his arms around* **Nell Nell**.)

Ferdia   You're soaking wet /

Nell Nell   and burning like a forest fire . . . who'd be a fifty-year-old woman?

Ferdia   Thinking about Tiernan?

Nell Nell   I should never have blackmailed Val to get his bail. He'd have been out by now.

Ferdia   I should never have blackmailed Val for the money to go to New York

Nell Nell Not you too! (*They laugh.*)

Ferdia   Poor Val.

Nell Nell   Fuck Val. I'm so proud of you for always refusing to be hidden, even at seven years of age.

Ferdia   There was two of us in it. Tiernan made me promise never to tell you but I was the one selling the magic mushrooms he got expelled for. He took the rap so I wouldn't lose the scholarship.

Nell Nell (*she cracks*)   Oh, Tiernan . . . he never could see his courage.

(**Ferdia** *hugs* **Nell Nell**.)

Nell Nell   Darling, you're sweating too.

Scene Twenty-Six: 'Foregone Conclusion'

(*Split scene: street/O'Rehilly Parade.* **Maeve** *carries her portable tape machine and mic.* **Dinny** *pops two Rennies in his mouth, grimacing.* **Ghost Young One** *drifts on.*)

Narrator   The sickness came out of nowhere /

Ghost Young One   **We all got it /**

Dinny (*winces with a pain in his gut*)   *Health was supposed to be a doddle after justice.*

Ghost Young One   **Some parents lost three or four kids.**

Maeve (*talks into mic*)   Families blown up and landing in no recognisable order.

Ghost Young One   **Grannies left rearing babbies.**

Maeve   Finally the Minister broke his silence on The Sickness

(**Maeve** *turns her mic towards* **Dinny**.)

Dinny   The problem isn't the problem it's the problem of the problem being made problematic that's the problem.

Narrator   And they would be the minister's final words on the matter.

(**Ghost Granny**, **Ghost Florrie** *enter, point out* **Dinny** *to the* **Future Ghost in Scrubs**, *who takes* **Dinny***'s Rennies and walks him off.* **Ghost Granny** *and* **Ghost Florrie** *smile and exit. O'Rehilly.* **Flix**, **Spangles** *and* **Tiernan** *enter.*)

Narrator   Flix and Spangles got hold of Tiernan . . . begging outside the Horse and Shamrock in Crickleburn.

Tiernan   *Nothing prepared him for the sight of* **Ferdia**. *He was a shadow of himself.*

Ferdia   Don't try and hide it whatever you do.

Tiernan   I'm sorry. I'm sorry . . . about Tom.

Nell Nell   *And Jimmy, Peter Fitz, Kenny and Joe* /

Ferdia   *dropping one after the other like toy soldiers. He wanted to say something philosophical . . . but the words wouldn't come out* /

Narrator   because he was twenty-five with a raging ambition for life. Unready and unbelieving /

Ferdia   *that the future could be so short.*

Narrator   There was no one to blame. Things just happened. Babies died. Hearts got crushed. Young men died in wars not of their making. It was the nature of things to fall apart /

Tiernan   *but not them. Not them.*

(Under the following **Tiernan** *lays* **Ferdia** *onto the sofa, and nurses him, stroking his forehead.)*

Narrator   It was Tiernan who found Ferdia collapsed by the stairwell, barely breathing and drenched in sweat.

Laid him down softly. All through the night they whispered soothing incantations to each other /

Tiernan *willing him not to succumb to it /*

Ferdia *extracting promises of a better life to be lived /*

Tiernan *as the heat of Ferdia's breath on his neck got colder and colder . . .*

(*The lights dim as* **Nell Nell** *joins* **Tiernan***; together they cradle* **Ferdia***.*)

Narrator The end came as quick as one minute falling into the next. And all the ghosts of O'Rehilly protested.

(*A riot of noise erupts, doors slam, pipes rattle, lights flash like when the curse is cast in Act One, Scene Four.*)

Narrator As the house itself keened for another of its unsung heroes took too soon.

(*During this* **Ghost Ferdia** *gets up and leaves the house.* **Players** *enter and pay their respects to* **Nell Nell***.*)

(**Ghost Bridie Meehan** *prays.* **Val Mooney** *awkwardly embraces* **Nell Nell***, shakes* **Tiernan***'s hand and leaves.*)

Flix *After the cremation, people were reluctant to leave Nell Nell /*

Spangles *knowing what was about to go down with Tiernan.*

(*A blue light flashes.* **Tiernan** *hugs* **Nell Nell***.* **Spangles** *and* **Flix** *walk* **Tiernan** *off into the blue light.*)

(**Ghost Bridie** *follows them to the front door.* **Nell Nell***, alone, goes to the window. Blue light and the noise stop.*)

Narrator For the first time ever, No. 1 fell silent.

(**Nell Nell** *senses it immediately. A woman with long white hair comes out of the shadows,* **Nell Nell** *turns: she knows who she is.* **Ghost Hibernia** *touches* **Nell Nell***'s bracelet, they look at each* *other a long moment. The dissonant notes and soothing breath sounds begin as* **Ghost Hibernia** *fulfils her wish and takes her daughter in her arms in the hour of her greatest need. The sound composition swells, incorporating all the sonic punctuation of the play in a sweeping, epic symphony of sonic shivers, typewriter keys, dissonant notes, trapdoors, footsteps and echoes.* **Ghost Hibernia** *leads* **Nell Nell** *to the typewriter, wraps a blanket around her, kisses her head and leaves. The symphony fades into typing as* **Nell Nell** *types,* **Ghost Bridie** *brings her a cup of tea.*)

Scene Twenty-Seven: 'The Finish'

(*Split scene: O'Rehilly Parade/Mount-of-Joy/street.* **Tiernan** *exits the Mount-of-Joy, glasses on, guitar on his back.* **Ghost Vincent Meehan** *watches him go. A* **Future Ghost Screw** *cuffed to a* **Future Ghost Prisoner** *enter.*)

Narrator   It was New Year's Eve when Tiernan Meehan walked free from the Mount-of-Joy /

Ghost Vincent Meehan   **two and half year served, his very own song-buke tucked under his oxter.**

Narrator   Stood at the prison gates /

Tiernan   a life without Ferdia rolling down the hill in front of him /

Narrator   His promise to his brother scorched across his heart.

Future Ghost Prisoner   Ah here, you're 'Nothing Squared'! My old fella has all your albums.

Tiernan (*smiles*)   'Nothing Squared' . . . (*Makes the connection.*) Yeah. That's me.

Future Ghost Prisoner (*as he's dragged off*)   **Legend!**

Narrator   Bound for O'Rehilly, Du-bb-ell-in had other
ideas. The city swept him up, laughing at and with itself, it
carried him down Carnell Street past monuments to the
ill-remembered and long- forgotten /

Tiernan (*looks upward*)   *down to the statue in the*
mouth of the street.

Narrator   Looking up at the great bronze hero crowned
with birdshit, he saw for the first time that /

Tiernan   *Nathaniel Carnell*
was the spitting image of Ferdia.

Narrator   A peal of his brother's laughter echoed on the
salty east wind cutting upriver.

Tiernan   *He knew then Ferdia would never let him leave* /

Narrator   forcing
him to keep his promise /

Tiernan   *There were songs to be sung here by people who had*
something to say.

(*O'Rehilly.* **Nell Nell** *types. One by one, all the* **Ghosts** *begin*
to populate the house. **Ghost Bridie** *gathers her bits in a sheet.*
Ghost Ned *climbs up toward the attic.* **Nell Nell**, *now*
co-creating with the ghosts, mouthing their words as they speak
and she types the final paragraph of her book.)

Narrator   Nell Nell had served out Tiernan's sentence
at her typewriter. An amanuensis no more, the words the
author wrote were hers /

Nell Nell   *because if she couldn't make sense of a*
world without Ferdia how would Tiernan ever do it?

Narrator   Writing allowed her to be someone else /

Nell Nell   and
herself /

Narrator/Nell Nell   at the same time.

Nell Nell   Words poured out of her faster than she could type, the book writing itself. It saved her from drowning in her loss.

Ghost Bridie   Sure the price of living was losing /

Ghost Ned (*leaving*)   **everyone you loved and everything you had**.

Nell Nell   Soon the house itself would be gone. Another echo of the past fading into nothing. A curse broken.

Ghost Bridie   The ghosts cast into the city streets, to wander where they would

Nell Nell   They were the air and the water /

Ghost Ned   **the dust and dirt** /

Ghost Bridie   an unlit lamppost, a scribble on a wall.

Nell Nell   The dead were everywhere.

(**Players** *fill the stage, the living, the dead, the future ghosts.* **Ghost Ned** *leaves the house.*)

Nell Nell   The city itself was not a building, nor a bar nor an argument of houses. It was its people, those who went before, all who walked there now and those yet to come.

(**Nell Nell** *tidies her huge manuscript.* **Tiernan** *enters, looks up at the house but doesn't go in; he waits outside.*)

Nell Nell   And so finished her story, for want of a better name she called it 'Dublin Gothic'.

(**Nell Nell** *joins the waiting* **Tiernan***; they hug. Then, holding hands, they mingle with the living/dead/yet-to-come.*)

Ghost Bridie   Never turned her dial back for a last look at the house.

Ghost Vincent Meehan   For there was more living and dying to do /

Ghost Florrie   and wishes to be spent /

Ghost Bridie   Until the time came to linger no more, in life nor death nor memory.

Ghost Ned   The time to be forgotten, to gladly take the open road /

Ghost Misfortunate   and find refuge /

All   *in Oblivion . . .*

*The **Players** all look outward in curiosity or wonder. Blackout.*

The End.

www.ingramcontent.com/pod-product-compliance
Lightning Source LLC
Chambersburg PA
CBHW041922090426
42741CB00020B/3453